CITYSPOTS

TURIN

**Barbara Radcliffe Rogers
and Stillman Rogers**

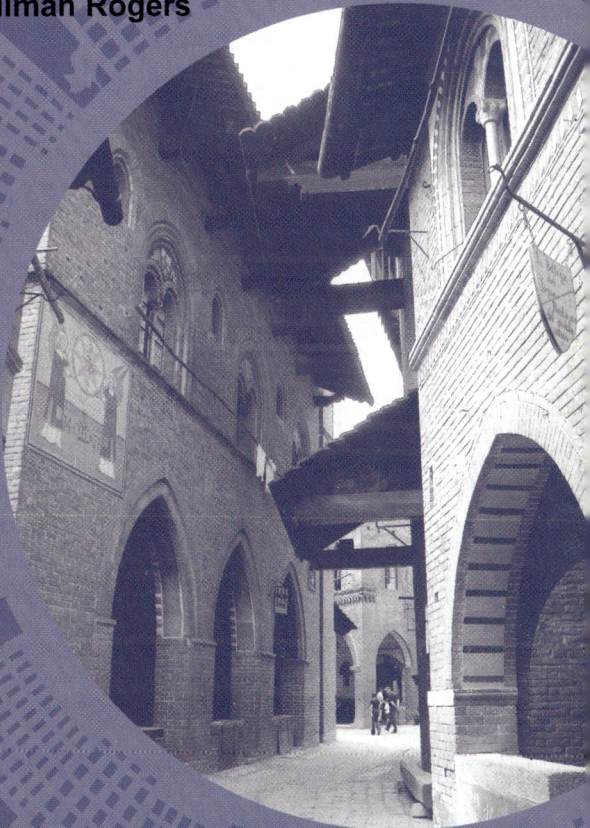

Written and photographed by Barbara Radcliffe Rogers & Stillman Rogers
Front cover photograph courtesy of Martin Lladó / Lonely Planet Images

Produced by 183 Books
Design/layout/maps: Chris Lane and Lee Biggadike
Editorial/project management: Stephen York

Published by Thomas Cook Publishing
A division of Thomas Cook Tour Operations Limited
PO Box 227, Units 15/16, Coningsby Road
Peterborough PE3 8SB, United Kingdom
email: books@thomascook.com
www.thomascookpublishing.com
+44 (0) 1733 416477

First edition © 2006 Thomas Cook Publishing
Text © 2006 Thomas Cook Publishing
Transport map © 2006 Communicarta Ltd
Other maps © 2006 Thomas Cook Publishing
ISBN-13: 978-1-84157-554-4
ISBN-10: 1-84157-554-2
Head of Thomas Cook Publishing: Chris Young
Project Editor: Kelly Anne Pipes
Production/DTP: Steven Collins

Printed and bound in Spain by GraphyCems

CONTENTS

INTRODUCING TURIN

Introduction 6

When to go 8

The 2006 Winter Olympic

  Games 12

History 14

Lifestyle 16

Culture 18

MAKING THE MOST OF TURIN

Shopping 22

Eating & drinking 24

Entertainment & nightlife 28

Sport & relaxation 30

Accommodation 32

The best of Turin 38

Something for nothing 42

When it rains 44

On arrival 46

THE CITY OF TURIN

The Savoy Centre.......................56

The Quadrilatero &

  Cittadella 72

Along the Po 94

Royal Palaces.............................113

OUT OF TOWN TRIPS

The Olympic mountain

  towns...116

Gran Paradiso &

  the Val d'Aosta.....................128

PRACTICAL INFORMATION

Directory....................................142

Useful phrases 154

Emergencies 156

INDEX 158

MAP LIST

Turin city map 50

Turin transport map................53

The Savoy Centre 57

The Quadrilatero &

  Cittadella 73

Along the Po...............................95

The Olympic mountain

  towns 117

Gran Paradiso &

  the Val d'Aosta.....................129

SYMBOLS & ABBREVIATIONS

The following symbols are used throughout the book:

☏ telephone	✆ fax	✉ email	ⓦ website address
ⓐ address	◔ opening times	ⓝ public transport connections

Hotels and restaurants are graded by approximate price as follows:
€ budget price **€€** mid-range price **€€€** expensive

24-HOUR CLOCK

All times in this book are given in the 24-hour clock system used widely in Europe and in most international transport timetables.

● *The Alps provide a striking background for the Mole Antonelliana*

Introduction

Turin comes as a surprise to those who know Italy – and to those
who think they do

No winding warrens of medieval streets (its medieval quarter
was built in the 1860s), no red sauce on the pasta (well, not very
often), no long midday lull, no crying violins or tenors belting out *O
Sole Mio*. Turin's favourite espresso is laced with chocolate (a civic
passion) and its café scene is more like that of Vienna than of
Florence. This is not the Italy of Tuscan sun and OAP coach tours.

This is the city where fast cars and Slow Food were born, where
Michelangelo never set foot (Juvarra and Guarini are the names to
know), where the Risorgimento (see page 15) is better known than
the Renaissance, where Minis raced through the arcades and
avenues in *The Italian Job*, and where the debated Holy Shroud and
gay pride co-exist in relative peace.

For all its differences, you would never mistake Turin for anything
but intensely Italian. The daily *passeggiata* – early evening stroll –is
alive and well, even in a city whose car manufacturing heritage leads
to images of Detroit-on-the-Po. The Italian passion for food here
takes the form of a reverence for fresh, locally produced ingredients,
which include truffles, rice, delectable salamis and Barolo wine.

In place of the winding cobbled streets, broad avenues spill out
into elegant and graceful piazze, both lined by miles of arched
porticos. Although built in different eras and in somewhat different
styles, these arcades give the city a satisfying harmony that ties
together its exciting architectural past and future.

The names of architects seem to slip off the Turinese tongue
with the same currency and respect as those of rock stars or football
heroes, and once you've seen the exciting works of Renzo Piano,

Marrio Botta and their compatriots you'll understand why. The startling transformation of the Lingotto building is a landmark of contemporary design – inside and out.

And for every Old Master on the walls of its formidable number of art museums and galleries, you will see a dozen pieces of modern art, from works of the greats – Paul Klee and Picasso – to those of artists just hitting their stride and others on the cutting edge of tomorrow's trends.

For Turin revels in the unexpected, and despite its rich history (or maybe because of it) takes pride in its edgy contemporary outlook. This is Italy with an attitude.

▲ *Piazza Castello is enchanting when night falls*

When to go

For the climate you associate with sunny Italy, visit between April and October. Take an umbrella, but expect balmy days. These become even balmier in late July and by August the heat is so oppressive that locals decamp to the mountains or the sea. August is a time to avoid the city. Although the weather is cooler in the mountains, hotels are filled with city escapees. Between November and March, Turin is downright cold, with wind sweeping down from the Alps and a dense clammy fog settling in for a week at a time. Snow is not common in the city, falling instead on the mountain ski trails, accumulating enough to make skiing possible through spring.

ANNUAL EVENTS

January
Linguaggi Jazz Concerts of different styles of jazz in various venues, featuring some of the best contemporary international artists. ⓐ Via Pomba 4. ⓣ 011.884.477. ⓦ www.centrojazztorino.it

February
Battaglia delle Arance (Battle of the Oranges) The three days before Ash Wednesday bring pageants, parades in medieval clothing and orange-throwing fights between neighbourhoods. ⓐ Ivrea (north of Turin). ⓦ www.carnevalediivrea.com

March
Automotor Show Lingotto Fiere, Via Nizza 294. ⓣ 011.664.4111. ⓦ www.lingottofiere.it

CioccolaTò A month of theatre, music, film, art and food, all celebrating everything chocolate. ⓦ www.cioccola-to.it

April

Festival Internazionale di Film con Tematiche Omosessuali di Torino (Turin Gay and Lesbian Film Festival) Focused on films dealing with gay and lesbian issues. ⓐ Corso Principe Oddone 3. ☎ 011.534.888. ⓦ www.turinglfilmfestival.com

BIG Torino Held in even-numbered years, showcasing new and emerging art. ⓦ www.bigtorino.net

Il Gioco del Teatro Compares new theatre trends in Europe, with performances at Teatro Araldo, Teatro Garybaldi and Teatrino Civico. ⓐ Fondazione Teatro Ragazzi e Giovani, Via Industria 2. ☎ 011.437.9039. ⓦ www.fondazionetrg.it

May

Fiera del Libro Italian books are the centrepiece of this annual book fair, with events for children and adults. ⓦ www.fieralibro.it

June

Festivita Patronale di San Giovanni Battista June 24, the saint's day of the city's patron, San Giovanni Battista, is celebrated with processions, activities and fireworks.

Momenti Estate From June through to September, dance, music and theatre performances at sites along the Po River. Tickets: ⓔ momenti.estate@comune.torino.it ⓦ www.torinocultura.it

July

Traffic Torino Top world bands and emerging local talent join in this annual festival of jazz, rock, techno and acid jazz. Free concerts and performances, but on first-come, first-served basis at indoor events. ☎ 800.015.475. ⓦ www.trafficfestival.com

Burattini Al Borgo July–Sept, Sundays. Compagnia Marionette Grilli presents live professional marionette theatre in the atmospheric Borgo Medioevale. Ⓦ www.marionettegrilli.com/borgo.htm.

September

Il Palio di Asti Horse race, preceded by a historical procession of people in medieval costumes, the local version of the Palio race that has made Siena famous. Held on the third Sun of the month. Ⓐ Asti. Ⓦ www.terradasti.it

Settembre Musica Among the most prestigious festivals of classical music, bringing top international musicians; recently added are nods to avant-garde, contemporary, jazz and ethnic music. Ⓦ www.settembremusica.it, www.commune.torino.it/settembremusica

Turin Marathon The 26-mile course is run through the city and suburbs. Ⓐ Corso Regina Margherita 497/23. Ⓣ 011.455.9959. Ⓦ www.turinmarathon.it

October

Fiera del Tartufo Bianco d'Alba Sat and Sun, early Oct to early Nov, with tasting and sales of intensely flavourful white truffles. During the event is Il Palio dell'Asino di Alba , where Alba pokes fun at Asti's Palio in its parody of donkeys 'racing' around the main square. Ⓦ www.fieradeltartufo.org

Salone del Gusto (Taste Fair) Takes place in alternate years, with the next in 2006. Among the world's biggest and most important food and wine events, held by the Slow Food Association (see page 24), with producer displays, tasting and sales. Slow Food information and links to the fair: Ⓦ www.slowfood.com, www.slowfood.it

Festival International Cinema della Donna The women's

international film festival showcases women directors and other women in the film industry. ⓐ Corso Raffaello 5. ❶ 011.440.7801. ⓦ www.festivalcinemadelledonne.com

November
Torino Film Festival Focuses on emerging directors, internationally. ⓐ Pathé, Lingotto. ⓦ www.torinofilmfest.org
Luci d'Artista Nov–mid Jan. An extravaganza of art in lights, by international artists; a typically Turinese take on Christmas illuminations. ⓦ www.torinoartecontemporanea.it
Artissima International exposition of contemporary art and the newest art trends. ⓦ www.artissima.it

December
Cappodanno New Year's Eve festivities include an open-air concert in Piazza San Carlo; reserve early for special events at restaurants.

TURIN PUBLIC HOLIDAYS
New Year's Day 1 Jan
Epiphany 6 Jan
Easter Monday 17 Apr
Liberation Day 25 Apr
Labour Day 1 May
Patron Saint's Day 24 Jun
Feast of the Assumption 15 Aug
Christmas Day 25 Dec

The 2006 Winter Olympic Games

Post-Olympic travellers can thank the 2006 Winter Games for some major improvements. Perhaps Turin would have built an underground transit system without the anticipated impact of 15,000 athletes and media plus a million and a half spectators, but there's little doubt that the prospect spurred them to quicker action. Certainly the nearly €100,000,000 upgrade of the airport at Caselle was an Olympic by-product.

Many buildings and venues created or remodelled for the games will go to residential or other non-public uses after the Olympics, but several will become sports or exhibition venues. Foremost among these is the old Palavela, whose 1960s hulk was revamped as the ice skating arena. Convention-goers will find it used as exhibition space after the medals have been bestowed.

Travellers following on the heels of the Olympics can expect plenty of lodging in Val di Susa resorts, where the newly-refurbished Valtur Village in Sestriere and Bardonecchia's Olympic Village will certainly translate into added beds. Many local hotels are getting a facelift, too. Although the brilliant system of shuttle buses from train stations to ski towns is unlikely to continue as a daily service, parts will probably remain during the busiest weekends and holidays.

MOUNTAIN VENUES

Sauze d'Oulx Freestyle, men's and women's mogul competitions.
Cesana Torinese Alpine skiing, freestyle downhill and combined, super-G, biathlon, relays, bobsleigh, luge and skeleton.
Bardonecchia Snowboard, giant slalom, half-pipe and snowboard cross.
Pinerolo Curling.

Pragelato Men's ski jumping, men's and women's Nordic skiing.
Sestriere Skiing: downhill, freestyle and combined downhill, special combined, and men's and women's slalom and giant slalom.

While it is doubtful that the names of 2006 Olympic venues will become household words of the magnitude of Cortina, St Moritz or Zermatt, their images on television screens all over the world will certainly bring new interest and more skiers. The world-class ski jumps and other sports facilities are sure to host future world competitions. It's a safe bet that these little resorts will no longer be almost private reserves of Turinese and Milanese skiers.

Turin's dream was to breathe new life into its post-Fiat economy by giving the world a reason to visit – and to come back. That dream seems likely to come true.

⬥ *Going for gold on the Olympic slopes*

History

The History of Turin – or at least that part of it that the casual visitor will meet – revolves around three factors: the Savoy family, Fiat and a succession of architects. Wrap these in the world's most famous shroud, and you've a bundle containing 90% of historic references you will hear. The Savoys and Fiat each played lead parts in Italian history; most of the architects are not household names – with the possible exception of the brilliant contemporary, Renzo Piano.

In the dim beginnings, a tribe called Taurini formed the village of Taurisia, prospering quietly until Hannibal crossed the Alps with troops and elephants (without today's tunnels, most of these never made it over the frozen passes) in 218BC.

Rome, on the make and moving north, rebuilt it as Augusta Taurinorum, a few bits of which remain today. On the fall of Rome, the city's fortunes from the 4th century depended on which northern invader came through, until in 1046 the local countess married Count Odo of Savoy, beginning the rule of the Savoy family. By the 12th century the city was independent, making its living from tolls on highways and travellers.

The Savoys gradually extended their local holdings, rising to a duchy with their capital at Chambery, France. Turin, meanwhile, grew rich enough to build a university in 1404. Spain and France fought over the region in the 15th and 16th centuries, but the Savoy dukes held on, finally moving their capital to Turin (bringing the shroud with them). They rebuilt Turin to rival the great capitals of Europe, much as you see its centre today.

The French again laid siege but the Savoys won out in the Treaty of Utrecht, which gave them the title of king. When Napoleon took a shine to Italy and controlled Turin, he left the Savoys in charge.

RISORGIMENTO – BIRTH OF A MODERN NATION

The Risorgimento, the revolutionary movement that lead to Italy's unification, spanned the years from 1815 to 1871. It began as Napoleon's reign ended and consisted of a complicated series of battles, rebellions and outright wars, but the final result turned a group of disconnected and often warring states and cities into modern Italy.

However, the winds of revolution were fanned by a group known as 'The Four Horsemen of the Risorgimento', stabled in Turin. The Savoyard King Vittorio Emanuele II wisely sided with these rebels, becoming king of the newly united Kingdom of Italy.

At the turn of the 20th century, the industrial age dawned with Olivetti and Fiat and a fast-growing film industry. In the economic depression of the 1930s, Mussolini's fascists helped Turin business put down labour problems, setting the stage for later labour activism. When Italy switched allegiance from Hitler to the Allies in 1943, Germany occupied the city, whose factories made it a target for heavy bombing. Continuing labour strife made Turin the birthplace of the violent Red Brigades, whose murders and kidnappings captured 1970s headlines.

The city has again shifted economic footing as FIAT's fortunes changed; with the growth of cellular phones and wireless technologies, the whole region has become an important telecommunications centre. Turin's empty factories morph into modern convention and exposition facilities, capitalizing on the area's food, wine and arts reputation. With the 2006 Olympics thrown in, Turin is poised to make tourism part of a vibrant future.

Lifestyle

The Turin is an outdoor city, despite its share of murky weather, largely because of the 18 kilometres (11 miles) of arcades that cover pavements and provide shelter for the city's myriad cafés. You could easily think that at any time of day at least half the population is taking an espresso break or getting a head start on the aperitif hour.

The Savoys, who patronised their share of these cafés, also set the pattern for Turin's cultural climate, commissioning rising architects to design their new capital, building theatres and encouraging art and music in the fashion of the older courts of Europe.

After the royals came the automobile aristocracy, who may have set a different tone from the court's gaiety, but continued to support the cultural life of Turin. Although the Turinese may work hard, they play hard, too, and they play on the edge.

The city's reputation as one of Europe's most avant-garde cities

● *Typical Turin – an aperitif at a café under the arcades*

in art and music began a century ago, with the newly affluent bourgeoisie who built homes and even factories in the daring art nouveau style, and patronized contemporary artists, architects and designers to furnish them. Today it is the popular electronic music scene, as well as its stunning contemporary architecture, that put Turin at the cutting edge.

While regarded as dour by southern Italians, industrial, hard working Turin has been influenced by large numbers of Sicilian workers lured here from depressed villages by a steady income in the automobile factories. Thank this group of 'immigrant workers' for the many pizza parlours in Turin, and thank the newer wave of foreign workers for the increasing number of ethnic restaurants.

Its university has always had a free-thinking influence on the city, attracting and nurturing political thinkers and activists. It is not surprising that the Risorgimento began here and succeeded, unifying the many fragmented little states we now call Italy.

Turin is a Catholic city to be sure – don't suggest too loudly that there is any doubt about the authenticity of the Holy Shroud – but it carries on the liberal traditions of its past, too. You will notice a more live-and-let-live attitude here: Turin led Italy's emerging gay movement and is more welcoming to the openly gay and lesbian than any other Italian city. Along with gay nightspots, Turin has **Circolo Maurice** (❶ 011.521.1116. ⓦ www.mauriceglbt.org), a social and sports club that acts as a clearing house for gay, lesbian and transgender events and venues, and **Informagay** (❶ 011.304.0934. ⓦ www.informagay.it), a meeting place and information point for the gay and lesbian community.

Balancing their active cultural and social life, the Turinese enjoy sports, not only as spectators at Juventus and Torino (the team most prefer) football matches, but with active individual sports as well.

Culture

The Savoys established Turin's reputation as an arts capital. Much of their patrimony remains today, with entire museums, such as the Egyptian and the Museo di Antichita filled with the treasures this family collected and passed on to the city.

The Savoys are not the only family that has shared its largesse with the public. More recently the Agnelli family, of Fiat fortune, has opened an art exhibition space showing 25 paintings of their outstanding collection; a whole palace full of decorative arts was donated to the city by an antique dealer.

This tradition of patronising the arts extends to the general public as well. The Turinese are avid concert, opera and theatre-goers, and they honour the city's place as the birthplace of the Italian film industry with good first-run cinemas and a state-of-the-art cinema museum.

In addition, Turin residents patronise the art and design galleries that sprinkle among the shops of the Quadrilatero, Citadella and along streets such as Via Mazzini. The Fondazione Italiana per la Fotografia is based in Turin, and the opening of their new headquarters near Porta Palazzo in 2004 gave them room for major exhibitions. Their projects include the prestigious Biennale Internazionale della Fotografia.

Large exhibition spaces are devoted to the paintings, sculpture and photography of contemporary artists, whose work is encouraged and valued. To learn what's happening in the smaller galleries and the alternative theatres and small venues, browse the walls and the cafés around the university, north of Via Po. Check also

▶ *Turin celebrates Italy's cinematic heritage at the Cinema Museum*

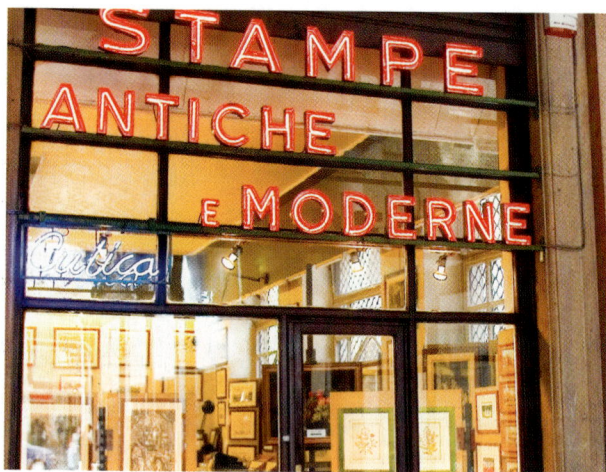

🔺 *Art lovers – and collectors – are well catered for*

the listings available at the tourist office on Piazza Solferino, as well as in Turin's daily newspaper, *La Stampa*. Its cultural supplement, *Torino Sette*, published every Friday, carries the most comprehensive listings. Or look for street stands with free *News Spettacolo Torino* Ⓦ www.torinospettacoli.it This website carries complete information on performances, with ticket booking details and prices,

The very useful Ⓦ www.extratorino.it and the official tourism site Ⓦ www.turismotorino.org both have English versions with details on venues and tickets and links to individual venues. The tourism site also shows the current special exhibits and programmes at galleries and museums.

▶ *Opportunities to shop abound, from chic boutiques to street markets*

Shopping

It has been many years since Turin let its claim as Italy's fashion capital slip to the catwalks of Milan, but cutting *una bella figura* – a fine appearance – is as important here as ever. Turin still has its own designer fashion scene and shopping – or at lease browsing in windows – is a national pastime.

Prices in the Hermes and Ferragamo emporia of Via Roma are high, but you can often find bargains on designer wear in off-price shops, such as Il Pallino (for shoes) and in the morning market in the streets around Largo Cassini. Along with Via Roma and Piazza San Carlo, Via Lagrange has a concentration of high-end shops. These and others in the main shopping streets are normally open from 09.00 or 10.00 until 19.00 or 19.30, with an hour or two closing at lunch for smaller shops.

For funkier clothing, shop the boutiques under the arcades of Via Po and the shops lining a solid kilometre of Via Garibaldi. Via Mazzini has a bit of both worlds, with trendy shops, but not quite such rarified price tags – and friendlier sales clerks. Across the river in Borgo Po, more highbrow boutiques satisfy the residents of the city's classiest in-town neighbourhood.

The Piedmont is well known for its distinctive food and drink: Arborio rice from the Po valley, Borolo and apertif wines, dried mushrooms, hand-rolled breadsticks and Turin chocolates are only a few of the delicacies travellers take home from this region.

Those who like their kitchens to be as fashionably dressed as themselves will love the variety and quality of culinary and table accessories. The whimsical and bright plastic accessories by Alessi are made nearby, so you can be sure of seeing their latest designs in Turin kitchenware shops.

Via Mercanti in the Quadrilatero is known for its fine craftsmen, and you can find hand-bound books and notebooks and fine letter paper here. In nearby Piazza Solferino is a venerable shop specialising in hand-finished candles. As you travel out into the mountain towns to the west and north look for typical alpine crafts, including excellent woodcarving.

USEFUL SHOPPING PHRASES

What time do the shops open/close?
A che ora aprono/chiudono i negozi?
Ah keh awra ahprawnaw/kewdawnaw ee nehgotsee?

How much is this?
Quant' è?
Kwahnteh?

Can I try this on?
Posso provarlo?
Pawssaw prawvarrlaw?

My size is ...
La mia taglia è ...
Lah meeyah tahlyah eh ...

I'll take this one, thank you
Prenderò questo, grazie
Prehndehroh kwestaw, grahtsyeh

Can you show me the one in the window/this one?
Può mostrarmi quello in vetrina/questo?
Pooh oh mawstrahrmee kwehllaw een vehtreenah/kwehstaw?

This is too large/too small/too expensive
Questo è troppo grande/troppo piccolo/troppo caro
Kwestaw eh tropaw grahndeh/ tropaw peekawlaw/ trawpaw kahraw

Eating & drinking

Everyone knows about Italian food: delicious, plentiful and hearty. But first-time visitors to Turin and the Piedmont may have some surprises. This region has its own distinctive cuisine, very different from the red-sauce traditions of southern Italy.

You're more likely to see cream-based sauces than tomato-based ones, and risotto may win out over pasta. Farm-fresh vegetables, mushrooms from the mountains, delicious local cheeses and trout are all products of the surrounding region. It was in the Piedmont that the Slow Food movement was born, and continues to gather advocates who shun both fast foods and those made with out-of-season shipped-in produce.

COUNTING EUROS

Food is a major part of the Italian experience, but it can be a pricey experience, too. Like city restaurants anywhere, those of Turin match their quality with high menu prices, although they are noticeably lower than in Rome, Venice or Florence.

One euro-stretching strategy is to shop in markets, such as the daily one in Porto Palazzo, for picnic ingredients (the local sausages and salami are excellent, and breads outstanding) and carry the results of your foraging to Giardini Reali, behind the palace, or to the riverside Parco Valentino. To dine with a view, hop on a bus across

---

RESTAURANT PRICE CATEGORIES
€ = up to €10 **€€** = €10–€20 **€€€** = above €20
(average price of main dish without drinks).

the river and picnic on the terraces of one of the churches overlooking the city.

THE MENU

What to order from the menu? First, remember that although it lists *Primi* (first course) and *Secundi* (second course) along with the *Antipasti* (starters) and *Dolci* (pudding), not all Italians order all four. No one will think it odd if you choose fewer courses – even one, as long as it is one of the two mains. If you like vegetables, order them from the *Contorni* list.

Local specialities include *bagna cauda*, raw vegetables with a rich sauce of cream, garlic and anchovies. *Agnolotti* are spinach-stuffed ravioli and *tajarin* is thin-cut pasta. *Brasato al Barolo* is veal braised in Barolo wine and a *fritto misto* here will be more meat than seafood. The region is renowned for its creamy *zabaglione* and *panna cotta* (crème brûlée) and for chocolate cakes called *torron*.

WINE WISE

Piedmont wines span the bounds of taste, from the fizzy party wine Asti Spumante to some of the finest Italy produces. Wine bars give you a chance to sample these by the glass without committing to a bottle. Look for the big bold Barbaresco, Barbera d'Alba and Barolo reds and Gavi or Roero Arneis whites. From the nearby vineyards of Lombardy you'll find the dry red Botticino and Cellatica, and the softer and more floral Gropello.

PRACTICAL DETAILS

Turinese dine late by northern European standards and many restaurants don't even open until 19.30 or 20.00. Lunch is served from 12.30 until 14.30 or 15.00. Select a dinner spot early and book a

USEFUL DINING PHRASES

I would like a table for ... people
Vorrei un tavolo per ... persone
Vawrray oon tahvawlaw perr ... perrsawneh

Waiter/waitress!	**May I have the bill, please?**
Cameriere/cameriera!	Mi dà il conto, per favore
Cahmehryereh/cahmehryera!	*Mee dah eel cawntaw, perr*
	fahvawreh

Could I have it well-cooked/medium/rare please?
Potrei averlo ben cotto/mediamente cotto/poco cotto, per favore?
Pawtray ahvehrlaw behn cawtaw/mehdeeyahmehnteh
cawtaw/pawcaw cawtaw perr fahvawreh?

I am a vegetarian. Does this contain meat?
Sono vegetariano/vegetariana (fem.). Contiene carne?
Sawnaw vejetahreeahnaw/vejetahreeahnah).
Contyehneh kahrneh?

table (or ask your hotel to do it). It is especially important to book ahead – at least a day or two– for popular restaurants on Friday and Saturday evenings.

The lines are becoming more blurred between *trattorie*, *osterie* and *ristoranti* – originally an *osteria* was a tavern that sold simple

▶ *Have a snack in opulent surroundings*

meals of local origin, in a less-than-fancy setting. Today, some are still what they were, but some very expensive 'country inn' dining spots call themselves an osteria, so you can't tell by the name.

Osterie and cafés usually stay open later than restaurants, which normally close the kitchen at 23.00. Many restaurants close on Monday and Tuesday, and those traveling in mid-August may have trouble finding any eating places open in Turin; this is when Italian cities go on holiday.

In most city restaurants you can pay by credit card, although smaller *osterie* and *trattorie* may accept only cash. Tipping, while appreciated, is not a fixed amount. A 10 per cent tip is considered lavish; €2–€5 is a respectable tip, depending on how fancy the restaurant is, and a 20-cent tip is adequate at a bar. Larger up-market restaurants may add a service charge, which should be mentioned on the bill, and no further tip is expected.

Entertainment & nightlife

Turin's club culture is the most avant-garde in Italy, and among Europe's most active. Spurred on by the university population, Turin's edge is grunge, centred around reggae, jazz and drum'n'bass, but including just about every known style from Black (Doctor Sax) to teenage bopping (Tuesday at Barcode). The action begins late – not until midnight at most places – and the venue changes with the season. In the summer it's along the Po, at Murazzi, and when the weather turns, the scene moves inland to Docks Dora, northwest of the centre. Traditional discos and clubs in the Murazzi begin around midnight and are usually open until 04.00, with some in the Docks Dora staying open until 06.00 (and even longer on Sunday morning).

Since the blast of Xplosiva onto European consoles, Turin and the Piedmont region have been getting international attention for their contemporary electronic music. Known as the Piemonte Groove, the best-known artists – those already on the charts and in heavy rotation on MTV and the networks – include Turin-based Subsonica, Gigi D'Agostino and Eiffel 65. Along with these attention-getters are even more underground and experimental groups and artists. Find out more about them and learn where you can dance to Piemonte rhythms at Ⓦ www.piemontegroove.com

Many of the Docks Dora venues belong to ARCI and AICS, associations that require membership for entrance. You can buy this at the door, but it may not be worth it for a few nights. Plead your case as a stranger in town who's heard how great the Turin scene is, and they'll probably find a way to let you in. Take a spare ID (not your passport) that you can leave at the door – and don't forget to retrieve it. Bars always have free admission, even when there's live music. Nightclubs and discos usually charge €10–25, depending on who is playing and how prestigious the place considers itself.

Turin is a city of music festivals, the biggest of which is Traffic in July, which brings in top performers – New Order, Aphex Twin and Carmen Consoli were among those in the 2005 festival – for free concerts. The list of live performance venues for rock concerts grew longer with the new stadiums built for the Olympics, and now includes the Mazda Palace, the Ruffini, the Lingotto auditorium, the Rai and the hockey stadium. Soon to join these is the projected €2million arena, seating 80,000 people.

With all the clubs and contemporary music on offer, it's easy to overlook Turin's long tradition of classical music, opera, ballet and theatre. Teatro Stabile is an umbrella organization where you can get information and tickets for both classic and innovative performances staged at several theatres (Ⓦ www.teatrostabiletorino.it). Teatro Regio is the place to seek opera, classical music and ballet. Dozens of other theatres showcase plays, comedies and cutting edge performances (Teatro Settimo is best known for these) and even marionette plays.

Turin is most closely associated with the cinema, as the birthplace of Italian motion pictures with the release of Pastone's *Cabiria* in 1914. New cinemas are opening and old ones have been modernised into high-tech, multi-screen complexes. Most impressive of these is the 11-screen Pathé Complex at the Lingotto. The Turin Film Festival in November continues the city's strong tradition of art films, and an entire museum is devoted to world cinema.

La Stampa lists performances with ticket information daily, but the best source is its weekly *Torino Sette*, published every Friday with complete listings. The Italian website, Ⓦ www.torinospettacoli.it has the latest updates on performances, tickets and prices. *News Spettacolo Torino* is available free from street stands, with performance listings and information on clubs and bars.

Sport & relaxation

The Olympic Committee could not have chosen a more sports-crazy city. More than three-quarters of the native population skis, 100 km (60 miles) of cycling paths criss-cross the city, and the first thing you will learn about a new acquaintance is their favourite football team – be it Juventus or Torino.

Paddle boats and rowing teams use the river, Parco Valentino is filled with weekend joggers and bicycles are used more for recreation than transportation. With world-class skiing less than an hour from the heart of the city, snow sports are so popular that schools close for *settimana bianca* – white week – in February so families can enjoy them together.

Runners and joggers will find lots of company in any of the city's parks, especially Parco Valentino, along the river, where the shaded paths are shared with walkers. But the best only-in-Turin running experience is on La Pista, the former Fiat test track on the roof of the Lingotto factory. The track is free to hotel guests – just stop at reception for a key, then take the lift for the art gallery and go through the glass doors to find 1.1 km (0.7 miles) of running surface. Each April Turin hosts one of Italy's top marathons (❶ 011.663.1231. Ⓦ www.turinmarathon.it).

The unloved Stadio delle Alpi, home of Juventus and Torino, is rarely filled except for games against Milan, Italian Cup or other title games. Buy tickets at the stadium or at the team stores: **Juventus** ⓐ Via Garibaldi 4 ❶ 011.433.8709, Ⓦ www.juventustore.com **Torino** ⓐ Via Allioni 3 . ❶ 011.521.7803. Ⓦ www.toro.it. You will need photo ID (passport or driving licence, for instance) when you buy the tickets, and you must take your ID and tickets to the game.

Outdoor swimming pools open to the public include Lido di

Torino (🅰 Via Villa Glori 21. ☎ 011.661.5210) and Pellerina (🅰 Corso
Appio Claudio 110. ☎ 011.744.036). An enclosed pool is at Centro
Nuoto Torino (🅰 Corso Sebastopoli 260. ☎ 011.322.448). Keep up your
training regimen, where there are weights and gym equipment, at
Playtime (🅰 Via Lagrange 27. ☎ 011.562.0520), .

On good weather weekends you can hire bicycles at impromptu
stands at major parks, including Valentino (🅰 Viale Ceppi) and
Colletta (🅰 Via Carcano), as well as at the Atrium in Piazza Solferino.
You can begin at Colletta, on the city's north end, and cycle along
the river and all the way to Stupinigi Castle and park to the south.

🔺 *From Fiat test track to running track – the roof of the Lingotto*

Accommodation

Hotels, ranging from cheerfully homely to state-of-the-art Euro-modern are conveniently scattered throughout the city, with some of the least expensive in the most convenient locations. Don't be surprised to find well-kept family-run hotels occupying the top floor of a fine old building, perhaps once a palazzo of lesser members of the Savoy court. Breakfast is often included, and may be a couple of bread rolls and a cup of coffee or may be an elegant buffet spread, such as the one at Hotel Victoria. Booking ahead is wise, since it will not only save you time looking around, but secures you the best price. Conventions often fill the city, making rooms scarce, another reason to book ahead. Weekend rates are often a bargain, bringing rates in hotels that cater to business travellers into line with far less luxurious ones. The Information office in Atrium Torino, at Piazza Solferino, can help find last minute lodging.

Turin is small and compact enough that any of the following hotels will be convenient to the sights. A surprising number of the lower and mid-range hotels are within a few blocks of the heart of the city, so there's little need to look for cheap motor hotels on the edge of the city.

City Hotel € Nicely located with suites, each has fax/modem plug in an attractive contemporary room. Parking available. Close to the Porta Susa station. Last renovated in 1995, this Best Western affiliate is among the best value in town. ➋ Via F. Juvarra 25. ➊ 011.540.546. ➊ 011.548.188. ➌ www.bwhotelcity-to.it

Ostello per la Gioventù Torino € Across the river on a hillside with views over the city, the hostel has canoe and kayak classes available.

ⓐ Via Alby ❶ 011.660.2939. ❶ 011.660.4445. Ⓝ Bus 52 (ask driver for the right stop).

Best Western Hotel Genova €–€€ Newly renovated, the rooms and public spaces are fresh and bright while retaining the charm of original 19th-century features. Reasonably priced parking.
ⓐ Via Sacchi 14/B. ❶ 011.562.9400. ❶ 011.562.9896.
Ⓦ www.bestwestern.com

Due Mondi €–€€ Well renovated in bright and attractive colours, this small hotel is close to the centre of the city. ⓐ Via Saluzzo 3.
❶ 011.650.5084. ❶ 011.669.9383. Ⓦ www.hotelduemondi.it

Hotel Artua & Solferino €–€€ In a convenient location a few steps from Piazza Reale, this family-run hotel is a welcoming blend of hotel and hostel, with a guest kitchen, in-room internet access, private baths, all on the top floor of a fine 19th-century building.
ⓐ Via Brofferio 3. ❶ 011.517.5301. ❶ 011.562.2241.
Ⓦ www.hotelartuasolferino.it

Hotel Continental €–€€ Bright and attractive decor marks the hotel, in a restored older building with nice details, close to Lingotto

---

PRICE RATING
The ratings in this book are as follows:
€ = up to €75, €€ = €75–€150, €€€ =over €150.
All are prices for a single night in a double room/two persons (breakfast usually included in price).

and Parco Valentino. Specials and weekend rates. ❸ Via Genova 2. ❶ 011.696.4537. ❻ 011.663.4592. ❿ www.continental.to.it/inglese.

Hotel Genio €–€€ Located next to the Porta Nuova rail station, the hotel has been nicely renovated to retain vintage details and add modern creature comforts. Amenities include modem hook-ups, and both cats and dogs are accepted. ❸ Corso Vittorio Emanuele 47. ❶ 011.650.5771. ❻ 011.650.8264. ❿ www.hotelgenio.it

Starhotels Majestic €–€€ Well located opposite the Porta Nuova Railway station, the hotel has been recently renovated to restore its original 19th-century style. ❸ Corso Vittorio Emanuele 54. ❶ 011.539.153. ❻ 011.534.963. ❿ www.starhotels.com

Boston Art Hotel €€ A mid-sized hotel that is well located, includes breakfast and has a car park available. It is decorated with original works of more than 38 contemporary artists. ❸ Via Massena 70. ❶/❻ 011.500.59. ❿ www.hotelbostontorino.it

Chelsea €€ This small, conveniently located hotel (near the Duomo) has been newly renovated and modernised. Rates are lower on weekends. ❸ Via XX Settembre, 79/e (Angolo Via Cappel Verde, 10122 Torino). ❶ 011.436.0100/1382. ❻ 011.436.3141. ❿ www.hotelchelsea.it

Conte Biancamano €€ With only 24 rooms, staying at this family-run hotel in the middle of town is like visiting friends. ❸ Corso Vittorio Emanuele II 73. ❶ 011.562.3281. ❻ 011.562. 3789. ❿ www.hotelcontebiancamano.it

---

❿ *Many of the hotels are right on the spot for sightseeing*

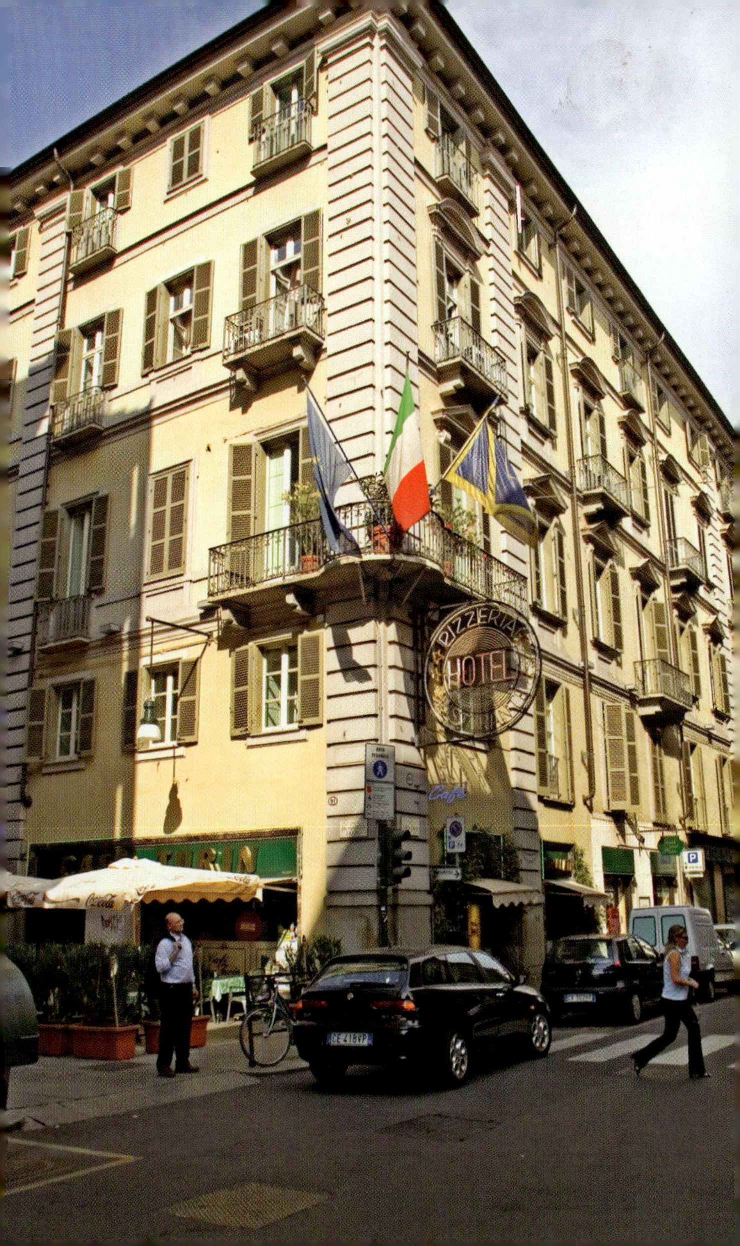
PIZZERIA
HOTEL
Cafe

Hotel Alexandra €€ Small and attractive, the hotel has all the expected room amenities. ⓐ Lungo Dora Napoli 14. ① 011.858.327. ⓦ http://alexandra.hotel-torino-hotels.com

Jolly Hotel Ambasciatori €€ Modern hotel in good location close to Porta Susa and Porta Nuova railway stations, the Ambasciatori offers good value for the amenities and facilities. Rates include breakfast buffet. ⓐ Corso Vittorio Emanuele II 104. ① 011.5752.
ⓕ 011. 544.978, toll-free from UK 0800.731.0470. ⓦ www.jollyhotels.it

⬤ The Hotel Ligure – a place for a jolly lunch

Jolly Hotel Ligure €€ The classic major downtown hotel is elegant, and close to theatres and museums. ⓐ Piazza Carlo Felice 85. ① 011.556.41. ⓕ 011.535.38. ⓦ www.jollyhotels.it

Liberty €€ This small family run hotel with a home-like atmosphere is centrally located between Piazza Reale and Piazza Solferino, in a *Stile Liberty* building (see page 82) . ⓐ Via Pietro Micca 15. ① 011.562.8801. ⓕ 011.562.8163. ⓦ www.hotelliberty-torino.it

Piemontese €€ You get a friendly welcome at this extraordinary art nouveau mansion, with all the modern hotel amenities. Rates are

significantly lower on weekends. ⓐ Via Berthollet 21. ❶ 011.669.8101.
❶ 011.669.0571. Ⓦ www.hotelpiemontese.it

Hotel Luxor €€–€€€ An independently owed Best Western
affiliate, the hotel is conveniently near the trail station, attractive,
comfortable and reliable. ⓐ Corso Stati Uniti 7. ❶ 01. 526.8324,
Ⓦ www.hoteluxor.it

Grand Hotel Sitea €€–€€€ A beautifully renovated classic hotel
with abundant amenities, just off Piazza San Carlo. Some special
rates can be a bargain. ⓐ Via Carlo Alberto 35. ❶ 011.517.0171.
❶ 011.548.090. Ⓦ www.thi.it

Le Meridien Lingotto €€–€€€ Also converted by Italian architect
Renzo Piano from part of the former FIAT automobile factory, this
Meridien has the former car test track on its roof where guests can
jog with a view of the Alps. ⓐ Lingotto complex, Via Nizza 262.
❶ 011.664.2000. ❶ 011.664.2001. Ⓦ www.lemeridien-lingotto.it

Meridien Art+Tech €€€ Strikingly modern, the Renzo Piano-
designed Meridien Art+Tech does as its name implies, combining the
best of contemporary art styles and the latest technology. Rooms
have work spaces and 30-inch LCD televisions, power showers and a
host of other gadgetry. ⓐ Lingotto complex., Via Nizza 230.
❶ 011.664.2000. ❶ 011.664.2004. Ⓦ www.lemeridien-lingotto.it

Victoria Hotel €€€ The elegance and feel of a country house, a few
steps from the central attractions. Each room is different and guests
have free internet and bicycles. ⓐ Via Nino Costa 4. ❶ 011.561.1909,
❶ 011.561.1806. Ⓦ www.hotelvictoria-torino.com

THE BEST OF TURIN

Whether you are on a flying visit to Turin or taking a more leisurely break in northern Italy, the city and its surroundings offer some sights, places and experiences that should not be missed.

TOP 10 ATTRACTIONS

- **Palazzo Reale** See how the Savoys lived (see page 62)

- **Mole Antonelliana lift** The view from the top (see page 94)

- **Cinema Museum** Film junkies' nirvana (see page 103)

- **Palazzo Madama** Roman stones and Juvara's stairs (see page 59)

- **The Duomo** Homage to the Shroud (see page 72)

- **Cafés under the Arcades** Hot chocolate or a *Bicerin* (see page 88)

- **Egyptian Museum** Simply outstanding (see page 64)

- **Piedmontese cuisine and wine** *Bagna cauda* and Barolo (see pages 24–27)

- **Stupinigi Palace** A little place in the country (see page 113)

- **Val d'Aosta** Gran Paradiso and Europe's Big-Three mountains (see page 128)

⬇ *The Piazza Reale is at the heart of Turin's sights and attractions*

Your at-a-glance guide to seeing the best that Turin has to offer, depending on how much time you have.

HALF-DAY: TURIN IN A HURRY

Savour the city on foot, strolling through its arcades (stopping for an espresso or *bicerin* in Cafe San Carlo or one of the other grand old Turinese haunts) and across Piazza Reale, stopping to look inside Palazzo Madama and to stand under San Lorenzo's fabulous dome.

If the Holy Shroud beckons, walk a few steps behind San Lorenzo to the Duomo to see its hiding place – and to glance at the Roman gate and amphitheatre remains, visible from the Duomo's steps. From there either continue west to wander into the little streets of the Quadrilatero, joining locals for an after-work *aperitivo* and free snacks at a wine bar, or head back through Piazza Reale and down the broad Via Po, stopping for *gelato* at Fiorio before veering left to the Mole Antonelliana for a view of the city and mountains from its glass lift.

1-DAY: TIME TO SEE A LITTLE MORE

The half-day intinerary, above, makes a good route for a full day, but you'll have time to tour one or two of the city's most outstanding interiors. Depending on your interests, this could be the Palazzo Reale – for a look at the grandeur that surrounded the Savoy court and to marvel at Juvarra's 'scissor' stairway – or the Museo Egizio, the world's finest Egyptian collection outside Cairo. Or pay respects to the birthplace of Italian film by visiting the Museo Nazionale del Cinema.

Towards evening, head to the Quadrilatero or on down Via Po to Piazza Vittorio Veneto for the apertivo-with-snacks ritual and dinner. If it's summer, use up your 24 hours by joining the late-night life of the Murazzo.

2–3 DAYS: SHORT CITY BREAK

With more time, you can explore different neighbourhoods or visit more sights around Piazza Reale, including the Galleria Sabauda and the Museo del Risorgimento Italiano, for a tour of the interior of Palazzo Carignano. Break the pace with a stroll in Giardini Reale behind the palace, and sample several more vintage cafés. Contemporary art mavens can hop a bus to GAM or to see some of Turin's best modern architecture in the newly revitalised Lingotto district. The Fiat factory-turned-shopping-centre retains its rooftop test track, with views of the Alps.

Museo dell'Automobile is, appropriately, nearby. Return along the river, through Parco Valentino and Borgo Medioevale. For longer views, cross the Po to Gran Madre di Dio, Santa Maria del Monte or take a bus to Sassi for the rack railway ride to Basilica di Superga (use your Torino card – see page 52). Or take a bus to the suburbs to see showy Stupinigi palace and its gardens.

For a relaxing break, cruise along the river Po (free with a Torino card) on the *Valentina* or *Valentino*, from Borgo Medioeval or from the Murazzi. Choose a different neighbourhood each evening for your *aperitivo*-grazing and dinner.

And make sure that you, at least one morning of your stay, hit the busy market at Porto Palazzo.

LONGER: ENJOYING TURIN TO THE FULL

With more time, you can spend longer exploring neighbourhoods, small museums and churches or take short bus excursions to visit the nearby royal palaces.

For a break from city life, make overnight trips to the mountains west of Turin or to the north, in Gran Paradiso National Park and the Val d'Aosta.

Something for nothing

Home of aperitif wine, Turin has elevated the aperitif-with-snacks to new heights. It may be the day's social highlight for hip Turinese, but for the traveller who brings along a smart outfit, it can mean free dinner. Wine bars outdo each other with spreads of hearty, sophisticated snacks to lure the after-work crowd. Cruise the back streets of the Quadrilatero and order a glass at a wine bar offering

● *Art under the arcades can be free (but he might expect a tip)*

the most interesting (and filling) food. Don't be shy about filling your plate – the locals aren't. For the price of two glasses of wine, you can eat a substantial meal, splitting your grazing between places with the best spreads. Begin early, while the selection is best.

It would be easy to spend a day or two in Turin without ever paying an admission fee. The city's streets, parks and *piazze* are living art museums, with sculpture, exciting architecture, murals, even pavement artists at work under the arcades. November through to January, the exciting Luci d'Artista illuminates the night with brilliant street art by prominent artists, all created in lights.

On the tourist-sight trail, tour Palazzo Madama free to see Roman remains and one of Juvarra's famous stairways. The Roman amphitheatre and Porta Palatina are free, as are examples of later architecture. Stroll art nouveau neighbourhoods and explore Renzo Piano's re-do of the Lingottto, with a scenic run on its rooftop test track. Return through the riverside Borgo Medioevale.

For views, climb the hills across the river to two lofty churches. All the city's churches are free, including Guarini's San Lorenzo, whose dome is among the world's greatest architectural feats. See contemporary art at GAM, free all day Tuesday; for a week in the spring, all public museums and monuments are free (Ⓦ www.beniculturali.it for dates).

Festivals mean free concerts, parades and activities, especially the religious/social feasts of Consolata on June 20 and San Giovani on June 24. During the latter everything closes and nighttime fireworks light the river. Carnevale brings parades, costumed revelers and street performers in the winter. For the price of a drink you can find live music or dance to DJs and in the summer you can listen to the music spilling from Murazzi clubs by just sitting on the river bank.

When it rains

With 17 km (11 miles) of arcades covering the streets, a little rain – or even a lot – doesn't stop the Turinese from the pleasures of window shopping and sitting in cafés. The sacred *passeggiata* goes on rain or shine, and the sidewalk tables of many of the city's beloved cafés are protected by the arcades. Along Via Po, these even extend over the crossings of side streets. Wide enough to accommodate pedestrians and cafés, those along the sides of Piazza San Carlo have pavements broad enough to serve as 'canvasses' for sidewalk artists, as well.

The shelter of these portici will take you, largely dry, the entire length of Via Po, between Piazza Reale and Piazza Vittorio Veneto, from Piazza Reale down Via Roma, through Piazza San Carlo and on to Piazza Carlo Felice. On the way there are two shopping arcades – one of them the refurbished 19th-century Galleria Subalpina, and the route passes the doorsteps – and shop windows – of some of the city's most prestigious stores. Via Pietro Micca, Via Cernaia and one side of Corso Vittorio Emanuele are covered, as well.

Turin adapts well to bad-weather travel in another way, too. Several of its museums are not only big, but varied enough to hold a visitor's attention for several hours. A rainy day gives a traveller the leisure to simply enjoy the moment, to spend a little longer looking at an exhibit or reading the labels. The Museo Nazionale del Cinema could easily occupy half a day with its exhibits, films and interactive displays, and even has a bar and café.

The 30,000-plus artefacts from the Savoys' hoard in the Museo Egizio, even if all are not on display at once, take time to see, and many short-term Turin visitors wisely choose to see those things more related to the city itself and leave this museum for a rainy day.

Likewise, the Museo di Antichità's multi-millennia archaeological dig is worth burrowing into at leisure, a pleasure it's harder to enjoy on a beautiful day.

🔺 *Chic shopping under the arcades: just the place to escape from a shower*

On arrival

TIME DIFFERENCES

Italy follows Central European Time (CET). During Daylight Saving Time (end Mar–end Oct), the clocks are put ahead 1 hour. In the summer, at 12.00 noon in Turin, time at home is as follows:

Australia Eastern Standard Time 20.00, Central Standard Time 19.30, Western Standard Time 18.00
New Zealand 22.00
South Africa 12.00
UK and Republic of Ireland 11.00
USA and Canada Newfoundland Time 07.30, Atlantic Canada Time 07.00, Eastern Time 06.00, Central Time 05.00, Mountain Time 04.00, Pacific Time 03.00, Alaska 02.00.

ARRIVING

By air

Small, modern **Sandro Pertini Airport**, locally known as Caselle (ⓘ 011.567.6361/2. Ⓦ www.turin-airport.com), is 16 km (10 miles) north of Turin. Its single terminal handles both arrivals and departures, with tourist information, money exchange, ATM and car hire all right at hand.

Taxis (ⓘ 011.996.3090) wait outside the arrivals hall, taking 30–40 minutes to the city centre, €25–40. In the same time you can take the train to Dora station for about €3 (ⓘ 011.691.0000. Ⓦ www.gtt.to.it), departing half-hourly from the station attached to the terminal's departures area. Your ticket is good for 70 minutes, covering a connecting bus to your hotel.

Buses (ⓘ 011.300.0611. Ⓦ www.sadem.it) leave the airport every

30–45 minutes 05.15–23.00, taking about 40 minutes to Porta Nuova railway station, with a stop at Porta Susa. Purchase tickets (€5) at either end of the route or on board.

Milan's **Malpensa Airport** is the best arrival point for travellers from outside Europe, and the €16.50 SADEM bus is the best way to get to Turin if your flight corresponds to its daily departures at 11.30, 15.30 and 20.30. These leave from Terminal 1, at Exit 4, Stop 18 (❶ 011.300.0611). Or take the easy shuttle to Milan's Stazione Centrale to catch one of the hourly trains to Turin, at the same combined cost.

By rail

Turin's largest rail station, **Porta Nuova** (❶ 011.561.3333. Ⓦ www.trenitalia.it) at Piazza Carlo Felice, links to all European destinations. It contains the usual big-city rail station amenities – ATM, news-stand, food, and a well-staffed tourist information point. However, Porta Nuova is being eclipsed by smaller **Porta Susa** (❶ 011.538.513), the terminal for the new Eurostar Italia route. The small **Dora** station (❶ 011.221.7835) serves the airport. Porta Nuova and Porta Susa are connected by Tram 1, and the new subway line.

By bus

Turin's bus station is at the corner of Corso Vittorio Emanuele II and Corso Inghilterra, about 600 m (0.5 miles) from Porta Susa (❶ 011.311.1616. Ⓦ www.sadem.it).

DRIVING IN TURIN

The best advice, at least until the subway construction is completed, is *don't*. Otherwise, Turin is a very easy city to find your way in, its grid design of streets alternating traffic directions and very few diagonal avenues to confuse the pattern.

Parking is a problem, despite new car parks in the centre and hotels normally charge extra for parking. Best to claim a rental car when you're ready to leave for the mountains. Routes in and out of the city are wide and well-signposted; get driving directions from your hotel if arriving by car. To find a parking space in any of the city's 18 multi-storey car parks, send a text message (SMS) indicating the letter 'P' to 339.994.9990 – the response will show a list of car parks with the number of spaces currently available in each.

FINDING YOUR FEET

Your first impression of Turin, once past the manufacturing suburbs, is how gracious and beautiful it is. Much of the centre is lined in arcades, lending a stately air and making walking a pleasure. Your first order of business should be to find a spot in a café under one of these and begin your acclimatisation to the pace of Turin life.

It is a fairly safe city, although you should always be aware of your surroundings in any city. Avoid walking – especially alone – late at night in the areas around the stations, Docks Dora or deserted areas. And better to save the amorous stroll in the park for daylight. Women will be hassled less in Turin than farther south in Italy. Fewer two-wheeled vehicles buzz in and out between cars than in other Italian cities and this makes crossing streets far less stressful.

ORIENTATION

A quick glance at the map on page 57 shows how easy central Turin is to navigate. Major attractions are close-set, connected by a grid of straight streets and broad piazze, so you could stroll past most sights in half a day. Plan your sightseeing to begin in the heart of the Savoy's capital, at Piazza Castello. Several major attractions are within sight of this wide plaza, and from it radiate four streets you will want to explore: Via Roma, Via Po, Via Garibaldi and Via Pietro Micca. If you lose your way, just ask in a shop. The only landmark you're likely to spot as a beacon is the Mole's sharp dome rising to the north of Via Po.

The maps in this book show all the main sights and streets in each area, but many of the restaurants, clubs and shops that we list are on smaller streets for which you will need a larger street plan. If you are planning to stay in Turin for longer than a couple of days, acquire a detailed map from a local news-stand, bookshop or the tourist office.

GETTING AROUND

A bewildering network of buses and trams connect all parts of Turin, many with a hub at Porta Nuova station. Ask at the airport

---

IF YOU GET LOST, TRY …

Excuse me, do you speak English?
Mi scusi, parla inglese?
Mee scoozee, parrla eenglehzeh?

Excuse me, is this the right way to the old town/the city centre/the tourist office/ the station/the bus station?
Mi scusi, è questa la strada per città vecchia/al centro città/l'ufficio informazioni turistiche/alla stazione ferroviaria/ alla stazione degli autobus
Mee scoozee, eh kwehstah lah strahda perr lah cheetta vehkyah/ahl chentraw cheetteh/looffeechaw eenforrmahtsyawnee tooreesteekeh/ahlla stahtsyawneh ferrawvyarya/ahlla stahtsyawneh delee ahootawboos

Via Guido Reni

Corso

Corso

Siracusa

Corso

Trapani

Corso Sebastopoli

Corso Lione

Corso G. Agnelli

Orbassano

Corso Ferrucci

Corso Unione Sovietica

Corso Mediterraneo

Piazza d' Armi

Corso a. de Casperi

Corso Selli

Corso G. Filippo Turati

Emanuele II

Centro Lingotto

Via Nizza

Stazione Porta Nuova

Via Nizza

Corso Vittorio Emanuele II

**Museo dell'
Automobile**

Corso Unità d'Italia

Corso Massimo d'Azeglio

Parco Valentino

Po

Corso Moncalieri

Corso Casal

N

0   500m   1km

Via Andrea Grosseto

Stadio delle Alpi

Via Badini Confalonieri

Corso Francia

Piazza Rivoli

Corso Lecce

Corso Potenza

Corso Tassoni

Corso Svizzera

Corso Francia

Corso Mortara

Via Cesalpino

Corso Grosseto

Inghilterra

Corso Regina Margherita

Torrente Dora Riparia

Stazione Porta Susa

Quadrilatero

Corso Venezia

Aeroporto di Caselle

Savoy Centre

Pza Castello

Giardini Reali

Corso Giulio Cesare

Corso Novara

Murazzi del Po

Basilica di Superga

information kiosk for a transport map, or buy one from any news-stand to be sure of the latest routing, since lines are changing as the subway system begins operating. Bus and tram stops are clearly signposted. Turin's new subway system, partly open for the Olympics, is not much use for sightseeing, but provides fast transport between rail stations and to outlying Lingotto.

Bus fares are €0.70, less for strips of 10. You must buy tickets – from any news-stand or tobacconist and in some bars – before climbing aboard. You might want a supply to carry you through Sunday, when many are closed.

Near the back of the bus or tram is a validating machine; insert your ticket with the Prima Validation side facing in. Tickets are good for 70 minutes of unlimited transfers, but can be re-inserted for a Seconda Validation. Most lines begin operating at about 05.00, running until 24.00, although not as frequently after 20.00.

Wondering when the next bus will stop? Send a text message (SMS) to 339.994.9990, entering the number (posted prominently) of any of the city's 3000 bus stops. In a few seconds a reply tells you the next arrival, in real-time.

The **Torino Card** combines free bus and tram transport with free admission to 130 major sites in the city and in the Piedmont, including the Mole Antonelliana's glass lift, the Sassi-Superga rack railway and boat rides on the Po. Begin using the card immediately for discounted airport shuttle. Although you may not take many buses because many sights are within steps of each other and many are free (such as churches – see Something for Nothing, pages 42–43), at €5–6.50 for major museums and palaces, three of these – only one each day – would make a 72-hour card (€17) a good value. Purchase Torino Cards for €15 (48 hours) or €17 (72 hours) at Turismo Torino Information Points or most hotels.

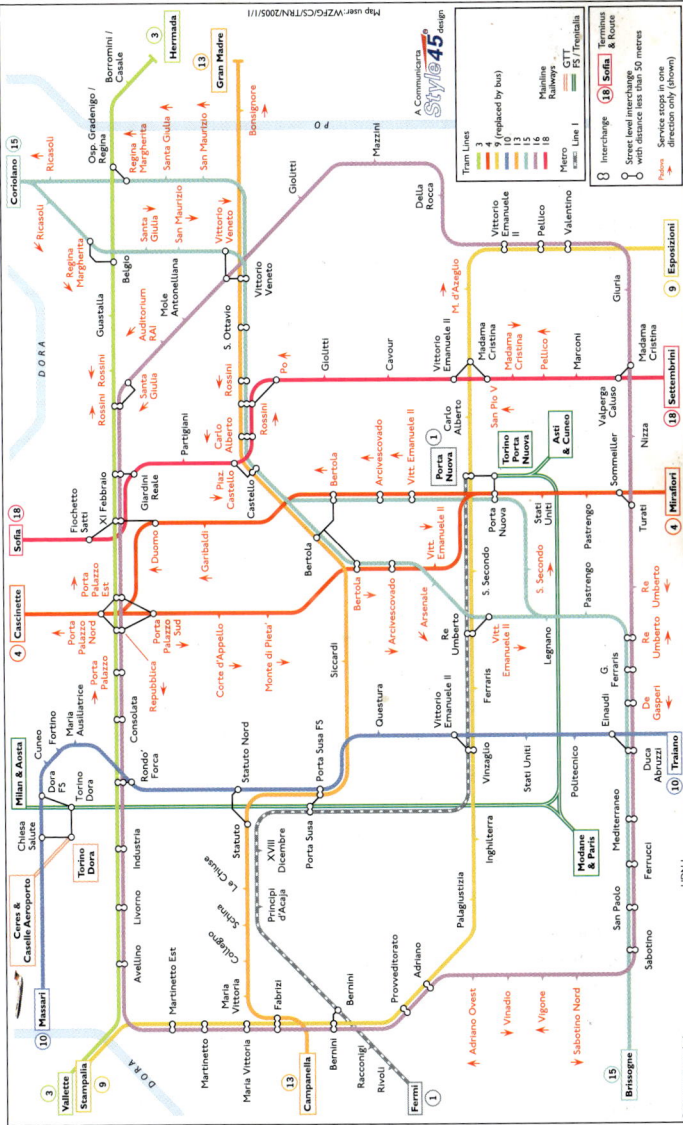

The **TurismoBus Torino** (free with the card) makes hourly circuits to 14 major sites, daily 10.00–19.00 from late June to mid-Sept, weekends and holidays in other seasons. Without a Torino Card, the all-day fare is €5. Although easy to use, its hours are limited and you may have a long wait for the next circuit. Those staying three days are better off with the Torino Card.

Taxis are plentiful, but you can rarely hail one from the street. Go to the nearest taxi rank (look for an orange and black sign), located at train and bus stations, major piazze and many hotels. Alternatively, call **Centrale Radio** (❶ 011.57.37) or **Radio Taxi** (❶ 011.57.30 or 011.33.99). All taxis are metered, with extra charges for luggage, night trips and if you call for a pick-up.

CAR HIRE

While you will not need it in the city, a car is the best way to explore the surrounding mountains. There are eight car hire agencies at the arrivals hall of Caselle airport. Link to these directly from the airport website, Ⓦ www.turin-airport.com Among them is **Europcar**, which offers some of the most competitive rates for Italy (❶ UK 132.422.233, USA 877.940.6900, Turin 011.567.8048). For quick comparisons, visit Ⓦ www.CarRentals.com Check rates before making your flight reservations, as you can often do best with an airline's air-car package.

Before leaving the car park, make sure you have all documents and that you know how to operate the vehicle. The main problem is for those from left-hand drive countries, such as the UK and South Africa. In normal traffic it soon becomes natural as you follow other drivers. But on roundabouts or dual-lane roads, it is more difficult. Stay alert and ask a passenger to remind you until it becomes customary.

▶ *Palazzo Reale: it's even more impressive inside*

The Savoy Centre

When the ruling Savoy family moved their capital over the Alps from Chambery, France to Italy in the 1560s, they wasted no time in remaking the medieval town of Turin into a glittering cosmopolitan city. Piazza Castello was arcaded and by 1584 work had begun on a swanky new 'suburb' laid out grandly along Via Roma. Spacious piazze and broad straight avenues became the hallmark of this area, which was further embellished in the baroque era. This grandiose urban sprawl was intended to launch their capital city – and the Savoys themselves – as forces of power and prestige. Thanks to Savoy ambitions, Turin became one of Europe's most regal and beautiful cities, and this former royal command centre is at its heart.

SIGHTS & ATTRACTIONS

This former royal centre is a place for a mellow stroll while admiring the arcaded buildings, broad piazze and gardens. A great many of Turin's sights are clustered around Piazza Castello, several of them in the royal palace itself, so you could easily spend a day visiting them all. But don't overlook the pleasures of joining the Turinese in just savouring *la dolce vita* in this quarter's cafés, parks and open spaces.

Piazza Castello

When Duke Emanuele Filiberto moved his capital to the small mercantile crossroads of Turin in the late 1500s, he at once began rearranging it into a modern city worthy of the Savoy presence. Although the shape and size of the square was determined by Emanuele's early architects, the piazza continued to take shape and form for the next two centuries, culminating in the baroque

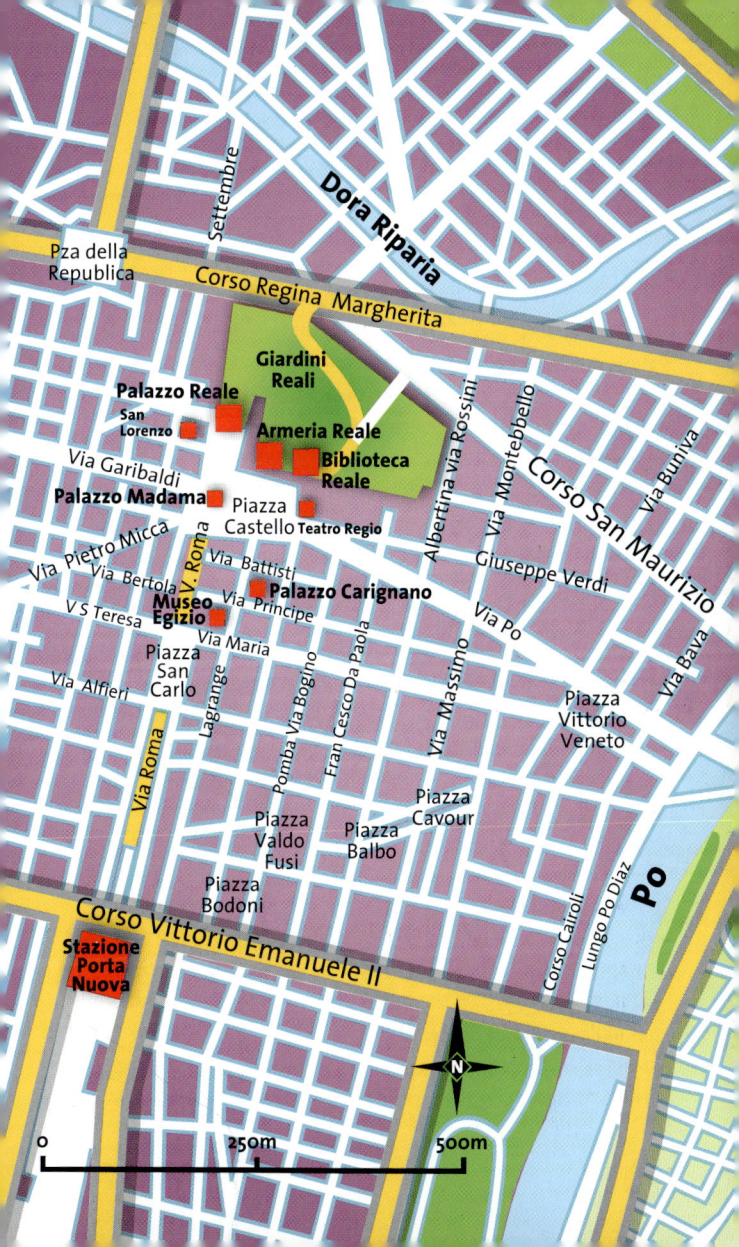

Settembre

Dora Riparia

Pza della
Republica

Corso Regina Margherita

**Giardini
Reali**

Palazzo Reale

San
Lorenzo

Armeria Reale

**Biblioteca
Reale**

Via Garibaldi

Palazzo Madama

Piazza
Castello

Teatro Regio

Via Pietro Micca

Via Battisti

Via V. Roma

Palazzo Carignano

Via Bertola

Via Principe

V S Teresa

**Museo
Egizio**

Via Maria

Piazza
San
Carlo

Via Alfieri

Lagrange

Pomba

Via Bogino

Fran Cesco Da Paola

Via Massimo

Piazza
Valdo
Fusi

Piazza
Balbo

Piazza
Cavour

Piazza
Bodoni

Albertina via Rossini

Via Montebello

Corso San Maurizio

Via Buniva

Giuseppe Verdi

Via Po

Via Bava

Piazza
Vittorio
Veneto

Corso Cairoli

Lungo Po Diaz

Po

Corso Vittorio Emanuele II

**Stazione
Porta
Nuova**

Via Roma

N

0   250m   500m

additions of Filippo Juvarra – the west facade of Palazza Madama and the state archives. Now traffic-free, the open space is studded with benches from which to admire the buildings. Ⓝ Bus/tram 4, 11, 12, 13, 15, 18, 27, 50, 51, 55, 56, 57, 61, 63 (note that lines 4, 11, 12, 27, 50, 51 and 57 stop here only on their northbound route).

Palazzo Reale (Royal Palace)

The palace of the House of Savoy was the nerve centre of the *zona di commando*, the command zone from which they ruled the duchy, and although it's a bit plain-jane on the outside, its sumptuous interior displayed all the pomp and grandeur of their position. The exterior makes up for its plainness in sheer size, with its series of buildings housing the armoury, library, archives and theatre, all connected by arcades. The palace was built in the mid-1600s. (See page 62 for the interior and tour information.)
ⓐ Piazza Castello. ⓣ 011.4361.455. ⓦ www.ambienteto.arti.beniculturali.it Ⓝ Bus/tram 4, 11, 12, 13, 15, 18, 27, 50, 51, 55, 56, 57, 61, 63 (note that lines 4, 11, 12, 27, 50, 51 and 57 stop here only on their northbound route).

Biblioteca Reale (Royal Library)

It is worth stepping inside just to see the vaulted ceiling. A self-portrait by Leonardo da Vinci is kept here, and occasionally on exhibit.
ⓐ Piazza Castello. ⓣ 011.543.855. ⓛ Tues–Sat 10.00–17.00.
Ⓝ Bus/tram 4, 11, 12, 13, 15, 18, 27, 50, 51, 55, 56, 57, 61, 63 (note that lines 4, 11, 12, 27, 50, 51 and 57 stop here only on their northbound route).

Giardini Reali (Royal Gardens)

Designed at the close of the 17th century by the same landscape artist as those at Versailles (the Savoys were influenced in their choices by the French court), the upper gardens contain a fountain full of tritons and sea nymphs. The intimate and charming lower gardens are accessible from another entrance, off Corso San Maurizio or from Viale 1 Maggio.

🅐 Entrance on Viale Luzio. 🕐 Daily 09.00–1 hr before sunset.
Ⓝ Bus/tram 4, 11, 12, 13, 15, 18, 27, 50, 51, 55, 56, 57, 61 and 63 (note that lines 4, 11, 12, 27, 50, 51 and 57 stop here only on their northbound route).

Chiesa di San Lorenzo (Church of San Lorenzo)

Guarino Guarini designed the church, whose austere exterior (like that of the palace it adjoins) gives no clue to the riot of baroque inside, nor to its interior shape. Although often hastily described as octagonal, its round-domed centre is actually surrounded by eight curved bays. Considered one of the world's great churches architecturally, San Lorenzo's fame rests in its dome and lantern, which is carried aloft on a delicate cage of intersecting ribs. It was described by one Guarini scholar as 'a great work of hallucinatory engineering'. Those who couldn't care less about architecture can't help but notice the exuberant baroque altar.

🅐 Piazza Castello; ☎ 011.4361.527. 🕐 Mon–Sat 07.30–12.00, 16.00–19.30; Sun 09.00–13.00, 16.00–19.30, 20.30–22.00. Ⓝ Bus/tram 4, 11, 12, 13, 15, 18, 27, 50, 51, 55, 56, 57, 61, 63 (note that lines 4, 11, 12, 27, 50, 51 and 57 stop here only on their northbound route).

Palazzo Madama

Think of this building – which you can hardly miss in the centre of the piazza – as one-stop shopping for the history of Turinese architecture. Beginning with the towers of the Roman Porta Pretoria, it includes a 15th-century Castle of Ludovico D'Acaja (on the Po River side), a baroque western facade and grand staircase, capped

off by a tower of unmistakable Fascist design added in the 1930s. All it needs to bring it up-to-date is another accretion by Renzo Piano in honour of the Olympics. However incongruous, it is a striking building, and you can just walk in whenever the doors are open to see the inside and learn more about its history from a free video. Highlights are Roman remains and Filippo Juvarra's grand staircase.

ⓐ Piazza Castello. ⓣ 011.4429.912. ⓛ Tues–Fri, Sun 10.00–20.00, Sat 10.00–23.00. ⓝ Bus/tram 4, 11, 12, 13, 15, 18, 27, 50, 51, 55, 56, 57, 61, 63 (note that lines 4, 11, 12, 27, 50, 51 and 57 stop here only on their northbound route).

Palazzo Carignano

Designed by the baroque master architect Guarino Guarini, the massive palace is made of bricks fired in a kiln right at the construction site, so Guarini would have just the right shapes for the curving facade. Look for designs inspired by tales of American Indians recounted to the Savoy court by a contemporary adventurer. The first king of United Italy, Victor Emanuele II, was born here, and the palace contains the chamber of deputies where the first Italian Parliament met. (See Risorgimento Museum, page 64.)

ⓐ Via Accademia delle Scienze 5 (off Via Lagrange). ⓣ 011.5641.711. ⓝ Bus/tram 4, 11, 12, 13, 15, 18, 27, 50, 51, 55, 56, 57, 61, 63 (note that lines 4, 11, 12, 27, 50, 51 and 57 stop here only on their northbound route).

Piazza San Carlo

Lined up perfectly with Piazza Castello, this is the second of the grand squares of the old Savoy centre. Three sides are framed in arcades, and the fourth maintains this symmetry with a matched pair of church

▶ *Duke Emanuele Filiberto rides across Piazza San Carlo*

facades, San Carlo Borromeo and Santa Cristina. In the centre of the piazza stands a statue of Duke Emanuele Filiberto on horseback, after his 1557 victory at San Quentino. Under the arcades are two of Turin's most famous and elegant cafés (see pages 66 and 68).

Ⓝ Bus/tram 1, 4, 9, 11, 12, 15, 18, 50, 51, 55, 56, 61, 67, 68 (note that several of these stop only on their north- or southbound routes).

Via Po

Wide enough for three carriages to ride abreast, Via Po was a marvel of its day. Arcades protect pedestrians on either side, even extending over crossings of side streets. Above them rises a uniform line of three-storey buildings, all the result of a strict city planning requirement of Carlo Emanuele's court architect. Peek into the courtyard of the university as you pass number 15.

Ⓝ Bus/tram 1, 4, 9, 11, 12, 15, 18, 50, 51, 55, 56, 61, 67, 68 (note that several of these stop only on their north- or southbound routes).

CULTURE

Inside some of the buildings mentioned above, and others in the Savoy centre, are museums that house Turin's artistic and historic treasures. Some are for enthusiasts of the subject – ancient Egypt, antique weaponry, the Risorgimento – and others are palaces that illuminate court life in the glory days of the Savoys.

Palazzo Reale

Inside the simple exterior awaits an almost overwhelming display of baroque courtly splendour, befitting the lordly Savoys. The palace's *piano nobile* (main floor) is open only by guided tours in Italian, but signs in English describe the contents of the rooms – if you can read as fast as the guides can talk. The Salone degli Svizzeri, the hang-out of the palace's Swiss Guards, is decorated with frescoes (the work of Giovanni Francesco and Antonio Fea) portraying the Savoy family genealogy. The ballroom is encrusted with decoration, its ceiling covered in a fresco of Olympus. This opulence is echoed in the smaller, but hardly intimate throne room, where band after band of ornate cornice moulding frames the ceiling. The crowning artistic achievement of the palace is the Scala delle Forbici, Juvarra's 'scissor' stairway.

Ⓐ Piazza Castello. Ⓣ 011.4361.455. Ⓦ www.ambienteto.arti. beniculturali.it Ⓛ Tues–Sun 08.30–19.30; visits by guided tour only, last tour begins 18.15. Ⓜ Bus/tram 4, 11, 12, 13, 15, 18, 27, 50, 51, 55, 56, 57, 61, 63 (note that lines 4, 11, 12, 27, 50, 51 and 57 stop here only on their northbound route).

Armeria Reale (Royal Armoury)

Displayed in a section of the Palazzo Reale is one of the finest collections of weaponry and armour in all Europe. Look here for the equine armour worn by Emanuele Filiberto's horse in the statue on Piazza San Carlo.

Ⓐ Piazza Castello. Ⓣ 011.518.4358. Ⓛ Closed at time of writing; check tourist office website for latest details. Ⓜ Bus/tram 4, 11, 12, 13, 15, 18, 27, 50, 51, 55, 56, 57, 61, 63 (note that lines 4, 11, 12, 27, 50, 51 and 57 stop here only on their northbound route).

Teatro Regio Tour

Backstage tours of the opera house include costume rooms, set storage, rehearsal rooms, the dome and the stage, where rehearsals are often in progress. This is a rare opportunity to see areas that are normally closed to the public.

ⓐ Piazza Castello 215. ☎ 011.881.5209. ⓦ www.teatroregio.torino.it
🕐 Guided tours (1.5 hrs) Sept–June, Sat 15.00. Ⓝ Bus/tram 4, 11, 12, 13, 15, 18, 27, 50, 51, 55, 56, 57, 61, 63 (note that lines 4, 11, 12, 27, 50, 51 and 57 stop here only northbound).

Museo Nazionale del Risorgimento Italiano (National Museum of Italian Unification)

Set inside Palazzo Carignano, designed by Guarino Guarini, the museum is worth entering for the palace itself, let alone the story of Italy's birth as a modern nation. A film in English does give a good background on the times, in which the ever-present Savoys played an important role. You can also see the room where the first Italian Parliament met, in the brief period during which Turin was the capital of the country.

ⓐ Via Accademia delle Scienze 5 (off Via Lagrange). ☎ 011.562.1147.
🕐 Tues–Sun 9.00–19.00. Ⓝ Bus/tram 4, 11, 12, 13, 15, 18, 27, 50, 51, 55, 56, 57, 61, 63 (note that lines 4, 11, 12, 27, 50, 51 and 57 stop here only on their northbound route).

Museo Egizio (Egyptian Museum)

Only the museum in Cairo has a more complete collection of artefacts from Egyptian civilisation before the sixth century. Exhibits, which range from state-of-the-museum-art interpretations to bizarrely random cabinets of curiosities, include a highly regarded statue of Ramses II and a collection of mummies and funerary finds.

ⓐ Via Accademia delle Scienze 6. ☎ 011.5617.776.
ⓦ www.museoegizio.org 🕐 Tues–Sun 08.30–19.30. Ⓝ Bus/tram 4, 11, 12, 13, 15, 18, 27, 50, 51, 55, 56, 57, 61, 63 (note that lines 4, 11, 12, 27, 50, 51 and 57 stop here only on their northbound route).

Galleria Sabauda

Paintings from the royal family's collections have been
supplemented by later gifts for a fine display, especially strong in
the Flemmish and Dutch masters, including Van Eyck, Rembrandt,
Van Dyck and Jan Brueghel.

🄰 Via Accademia delle Scienze 6. ☎ 011.4406.903. 🄻 Tues 08.30–
14.00, Wed 14.00–19.30, Thur 10.00–19.30, Fri–Sat 08.30–1400.
🄽 Bus/tram 4, 11, 12, 13, 15, 18, 27, 50, 51, 55, 56, 57, 61, 63 (note that lines
4, 11, 12, 27, 50, 51 and 57 stop here only on their northbound route).

RETAIL THERAPY

They're all here, under the arcades of Via Roma: Hermes, Fasano,
Promod, Gucci, Prada, Armani, Ferragamo. Unless you are dressed to
the part, and seem intent on purchase in some of these, you may
find sales clerks looking down their aquiline noses at you. Cruise
other neighbourhoods for more wearable and affordable goods.
Most shops in this area close Monday morning and all day Sunday.

RAO Strictly for the privileged set with a compulsion to also be well
dressed, RAO features quality women's clothing by top designers.
The male equivalent is nearby, at Via Andrea Doria 8. 🄰 Via Lagrange
at Via Cavour. ☎ 011.562.1298. 🄽 Bus/tram 1, 18, 61, 68.

La Bisaccia Accessorise here with scarves, fine leather handbags and
upmarket baubles. 🄰 Via Carlo Alberto 1. ☎ 011.817.0230.
🄻 Closed Sun and Mon afternoon. 🄽 Bus/tram 13, 15, 18, 61, 68.

La Rinascente Reliable mid–upper range department store.
🄰 Via Lagrange 15–17. ☎ 011.561.1577. 🄽 Bus/tram 1, 18, 61, 68.

UPIM An oasis of lower-priced clothing amid the Via Roma hautier.
🅐 Via Roma 305. 🕿 011.544.957. Ⓝ Bus/tram 4, 15, 63.

Donna in Campo It's a welcome respite from the relentless chic as women from all over the Piedmont gather here to display and sell traditional and contemporary handwork. 🅐 Piazza Carignano.
🕒 Feb–June and Sept–Dec, last Sun of the month.

TAKING A BREAK

Under the arcades of piazze San Carlo and Castello are the city's ritziest and most venerable cafés, and it would be criminal to visit Turin without sampling at least one of them. As much a part of Turin as Fiat and the Shroud – and to many, even more holy – the cafés are the weft of its gastronomic, architectural, historical and social fabric. Whatever table you choose, you can be certain that the elbows of an important musician, statesman, writer, artist or bon vivant rested there before yours – or will rest there next week.

Caffè San Carlo With the distinction of being the first café in Italy (maybe in Europe) to be lit by gas, this elegant café was the haunt of Risorgimento patriots, who nibbled the delectable San Carlo almond cake as they plotted. You can, too, while admiring one of the finest plaster work and gilt interiors in the city. 🅐 Piazza San Carlo 156.
🕿 011.532.586. 🕒 Daily 12.00–15.00, 19.00–23.00 for meals, all day for café service. Ⓝ Bus/tram 1, 4, 9, 11, 12, 15, 18, 50, 51, 55, 56, 61, 67, 68 (note that several of these stop only on their north- or southbound routes).

▶ *Stile Liberty – art nouveau style – can even be found in shops*

Caffè Baratti & Milano Best known for its aperitifs and lovely sandwiches, this Turin institution also serves lunch. It was a favourite of the Savoy royals. ⓐ Piazza Castello 29 (at the entrance to the Gallerie Subalpina). ⓣ 011.561.3060. ⓛ Serves lunch 12.30–14.30, café service all day. ⓝ Bus/tram 4, 11, 12, 13, 15, 18, 27, 50, 51, 55, 56, 57, 61, 63 (note that lines 4, 11, 12, 27, 50, 51 and 57 stop here only on their northbound route).

Fiorio Although some of the splendour of the decor may have faded, the gelato is as creamy as when the Savoys smacked their royal lips over it. Reputed to be the best cream *gelati* in Italy, a claim we can't dispute. Order their speciality – a three-scoop combo of chocolate, pistachio and vanilla. ⓐ Via Po 8. ⓣ 011.817.3225. ⓛ Tues–Sun. ⓝ Bus/tram 13, 15, 55, 56, 61.

Gertosio This neighbouring bakery and deli make such a good team that it can't be by accident. For a picnic lunch, buy bread at one and filling at the other. ⓐ Via Lagrange 34. ⓣ 011.562.1942. **La Baita del Formagg** ⓐ Via Lagrange 36. ⓣ 011.562.3224.

La Focacceria Tipica Ligure € For lunch on the run – and on the cheap – take-away pizza or a focaccia, called *farinata*. ⓐ Via Giovanni Gioliti 4. ⓣ 011.530.185. ⓝ Bus/tram 1, 18, 61, 68.

Arcadia €€ In the 19th-century covered shopping gallery off Piazza Castello, Arcadia is a handy lunch stop while touring the Savoy sights. Duck breast is paired with honey and peperoncino, lamb served with pear confit and veal is crusted in potato and sauced in red wine. For a lighter lunch, all the pasta is made fresh in-house. ⓐ Galleria Subalpina. ⓣ 011.561.3898. ⓦ www.ristorantearcadia.com

🕐 Mon–Sat 12.30–14.30 20.00–23.00. 🚌 Bus/tram 4, 11, 12, 13, 15, 18, 27, 50, 51, 55, 56, 57, 61, 63 (note that lines 4, 11, 12, 27, 50, 51 and 57 stop here northbound only).

AFTER DARK

Strolling through the arcades is the best way to begin an evening, perhaps with a stop as the Turinese do, for an apertif in one of the cafés. Buildings in this area are lavishly illuminated at night, especially the Palazzo Madama and others in Piazza Castello. Some of the elegant cafés, including the Caffè San Carlo (see page 66) serve dinner, another chance to enjoy their sumptuous interiors.

Restaurants
L'Agrifoglio €€ Traditional ambience and modern interpretations of Piedmont classics, including *agnolotti* (local ravioli) and rabbit.
📍 Via Accademia Albertina 9 (near Vittorio Emanuele end of street).
📞 011.837.064. 🕐 Tues–Sat 19.00–23.00. 🚌 Bus/tram 18, 52, 61, 68.

La Badessa €€ Dine amid antiques inside the noble Palazzo Coardi di Carpeneto, or outside overlooking the piazza, on dishes made from recipes from historic abbeys. The religious dined well, and so will you, on main courses such as swordfish with saffron rice cakes or grilled veal stuffed with fontina cheese and herbs.
📍 Piazza Carlo Emanuele II 17. 📞 011.835.940. 🕐 Tues–Sat 12.00–14.30, Mon–Sat 19.50–23.00. 🚌 Bus/tram 13, 15, 55, 56, 61.

Cinemas & theatres
Teatro Regio The two theatres in Piazza Castello, Teatro Regio and Piccolo Regio, present a wide range of musical events, including

opera, ballet, symphony and vocal concerts. Giacomo Puccini's *La Bohème* premiered in the Piccolo Regio. Opening nights need to be booked early, but tickets are usually available same day for other performances. ⓐ Piazza Castello 215. ⓣ 011.8815241.
ⓦ www.teatroregio.torino.it Ⓝ Bus/tram 4, 11, 12, 13, 15, 18, 27, 50, 51, 55, 56, 57, 61, 63 (note that lines 4, 11, 12, 27, 50, 51 and 57 stop here only on their northbound route).

Teatro Carignano Attend a stage performance here, even if you cannot understand Italian (although some are in English) to revel in the grandeur of Turin's only remaining theatre from the 1700s, almost entirely in its original appearance. ⓐ Piazza Carignano 6.
ⓣ 011.547.048, Ticket office ⓣ 011.5176.246/011.5637.079, toll free

⬤ *Hitting the floor at one of Turin's many lively clubs*

from Italy 800 235 333. Ⓦ www.teatrostabiletorino.it Ⓝ Bus/tram 4, 11, 12, 13, 15, 18, 27, 50, 51, 55, 56, 57, 61, 63 (note that lines 4, 11, 12, 27, 50, 51 and 57 stop here only on their northbound route).

Teatro Gobetti Prose theatre productions, occasionally in English, by touring foreign and Italian companies. Ⓐ Via Rossini 8. Ⓣ 011.8159.132; Box office: Via Roma 49. Ⓣ 011.5176.246/011.5637.079, (toll-free from Italy 800 235 333). Ⓦ www.teatrostabiletorino.it Ⓝ Bus/tram 13, 15, 55, 56, 61 (note that 61 stops at Via Rossini only eastbound – towards the river).

Romano Three small cinemas in one, showing current releases, mostly major hits. Ⓐ Galleria Subalpina; Ⓣ 011.562.0145. Ⓝ Bus/tram 4, 11, 12, 13, 15, 18, 27, 50, 51, 55, 56, 57, 61, 63 (note that lines 4, 11, 12, 27, 50, 51 and 57 stop here northbound only).

Bars, clubs & discos

Factory Café Stir fusion or acid jazz into your oyster martini at this trendy bar, where they also serve pizza and made-to-order sushi. Gucci recommended, but not required. Ⓐ Via Lagrange 21. Ⓣ 011.1971.0580. Ⓦ www.factorycafé.it Ⓛ Tues–Sun 18.00–03.00. Ⓝ Bus/tram 18, 68, 61.

Barrumba Look here for more cutting edge Italian rock and BritPop live shows, where it's more about the music: Mantaray, Stereolab, Super Furry Animals and Dodgy have all played there. Loosely based on the London club, but with a distict Turinese accent, Barrumba is one of the city's best places for whatever's hot in hip-hop, reggae, ska, metal, grunge, punk and jungle. Ⓐ Via San Massimo 1; Ⓣ 011.819.4347. Ⓦ www.barrumba.com Ⓛ Tues–Sun 22.00–04.00. Ⓝ Bus/tram 13, 15, 55, 56, 61 (note that these stop running about 24.00).

The Quadrilatero & Cittadella

While the Savoys' building boom reshaped everything east of the Duomo with new broad avenues and piazze, the area to the west was allowed to evolve pretty much on its own. So no one style dominates to the west of Via Roma. The city's oldest churches – and oldest structures of any kind – are in the Quadrilatero, where you will find Roman and the city's only medieval buildings. As you roam south into Cittadella, you'll discover remnants of the 1500s citadel, plus every building style since, from baroque to art nouveau and contemporary, in an interesting, eclectic jumble.

SIGHTS & ATTRACTIONS

The Duomo, which seems to turn its back on the Savoy command centre although it was very much a part of it, is a good place to begin exploring the area known as the Quadrilatero Romano. This extends north to Piazza della Republica, beyond which is the newly revitalised Docks Dora area. Via Garibaldi leads west, and to the south is the Citadella, former site of the 16th-century walled fortress. Here and farther south are some of Turin's most striking examples of art nouveau. The city's oldest churches – and oldest structures of any kind – are in the Quadrilatero.

Duomo di San Giovanni Battista (Cathedral)

Although the cathedral is best known as the location of the Holy Shroud (La Sacra Sindone), this religious relic actually has its own home, in a separate chapel between the church and the Savoy palace. But a 1997 fire seriously damaged that chapel and very nearly took the shroud itself. During the restoration, the shroud is

Oddone

Corso Lungo Dora Napoli

Corso Lungo Dora Riparia

Corso Lungo D Savona

Dora Riparia

Via Cigna

V. Borgo Dora

Corso Giulio

Cottolengo

Piazza Della

Corso Principe

C Pronc Fugenio

Via Giulio

Corso Regina Margherita

Pza Consolata

La Consolata

Piazza Augusto

Museo della Sindone

C Valdocco

Via Ortane

San Domenico

Porta Palatina

Settembre

Museo d' Antichita

Duomo

Giardini Reali

Piazza Statuto

Allioni

Passalacqua

Palazzo Falletti di Barolo

Corpus Domini

Pza S Giovanni

Via Garibaldi

Piazza Castello

Stazione Porta Susa

Corso Palestro

Cernia V S Teresa

Via Milano

Via Pietro Micca

Via Bertola

V Accad Scienze

Guicciardini

Via V Amedeo

Teatro Alfieri

Piazza Solferino

Via Roma

Via Maria

Lagange

Pomba Via Bogino

Fran Cesco Da Paola

Albertina via Rossini

Museo dell' Artigliera

Via Alfieri

Museo Pietro Micca

Corso Ferraris

Matteotti

Corso Re Umberto

Corso Giacomo

Piazza Valdo Fusi

Piazza Balbo

Piazza Bodoni

Corso Vittorio Emanuele II

GAM

Stazione Porta Nuova

0   250m   500m

N

housed in a side chapel to the left of the main altar; it is rarely on view, but a replica is displayed near the entrance to the church.

Above the entrance is a copy of da Vinci's *The Last Supper* commissioned by Savoy Duke Carlo Felice and presented to the Duomo by Carlo Alberto. In the second altar of the right is a noteworthy series of panels from a 16th-century painted altarpiece. The building itself is the only major Renaissance work remaining in Turin, built in the 1490s. The facade is decorated by carved marble panels that surround the doors.

ⓐ Piazza San Giovanni. ☏ 011.436.1540. ⏱ Mon–Sat 07.00–12.30 and 15.00–19.00, Sun 08.00–12.00 and 15.00–19.00. Mass: Mon–Sat 07.00 and 18.00, Sun 09.00, 10.30, 18.00. Ⓝ Bus/tram 4, 11, 11, 12, 27, 50, 51, 57 (all stop northbound only).

Teatro Romano (Roman Amphitheatre)

The Roman city was variously incorporated, removed, covered or left in place, so the area north of Via Garibaldi – the Romans' *decimus maximus* – still has some remains from that era. Among them is part of the amphitheatre, the rest of which was covered over by the royal palace complex. The open-air site next to the Duomo is fenced, so you can't wander about its ancient stones, but fully visible.

ⓐ Piazza San Giovanni. Ⓝ Bus/tram 4, 11, 11, 12, 27, 50, 51, 57 (all stop northbound only).

Porta Palatina

Near the remains of Roman walls stands the imposing gate, the only remaining of the four entrances to the Roman city of Augusta Taurinorum. Built in the first century AD, it is one of the best

---

▶ *The sumptuous home of the Holy Shroud*

preserved Roman gates in the world. Constructed of brick, it has two polygonal towers connected by a three-storey wall. During the gate's two millennia it has been used as a noble residence and a prison for women. Legend holds that the Emperor Charlemagne camped here in 773. The statues of Caesar and Augustus are not originals.

ⓐ Via XX Settembre. Ⓝ Bus/tram 4, 11, 11, 12, 27, 50, 51, 57 (all stop northbound only).

Casa Fossati Rayneri

From the Duomo, Via IV Marzo heads west at a southern angle, passing a rare sight in Turin: a medieval building. Look for the terracotta ornaments on the upper storey windows.

ⓐ Via IV Marzo at Via Porta Palatina. Ⓝ Bus/tram Duomo stop lines 4, 11, 11, 12, 27, 50, 51, 57 (all stop northbound route only).

Chiesa di Corpus Domini (Church of the Lord's Body)

The altarpiece depicts the story of a French soldier who stole a chalice containing a consecrated host from a church in Val di Susa in 1453, but when he tried to sell it in Turin, the chalice jumped from his pack and suspended itself in the air just out of reach. The spot where this happened was commemorated by this church a century and a half later, by which time the Duomo had already claimed the chalice. It remains there today, used annually on Maundy Thursday. The church's rich and colourful marble interior was completed in the mid-1700s.

ⓐ Piazza Corpus Domini (Via San Tommaso at Via Municipio); ⓘ 011.436.6025. Ⓛ Daily 07.30–11.30, 15.00–18.00, closed Aug afternoon. Mass: Mon–Sat 07.30, Thur 17.30, Sun 10.00.

Ⓝ Bus/tram 4, 11, 11, 12, 27, 50, 51, 57 (all stop northbound route only).

Chiesa di San Domenico (St Dominic's Church)

Turin's only real Gothic church, what you see today is actually more the late 1700s rebuild and early 20th-century restorations than the original of the early 1300s. The main altar dates from this period. Otherwise, the rebuild looks much like the church that was built for the Dominican monks, with its rose window and ribbed interior vaulting. In the Capella della Madonna delle Grazie are the original frescoes painted from 1350 to 1360, the city's oldest and only survivor from that period.

🚇 Via San Domenico (corner of Via Milano). ☎ 011.522.9711. 🕐 Daily 07.00–12.00, 1600–18.30. Mass: Mon–Fri 07.30 and 18.30, Sun 10.00 and 18.00. 🚌 Bus/tram 4, 11, 12, 27, 57 (all stop southbound only).

Piazza Consolata

A small square, but a busy one, with perhaps the city's best loved – and busiest – church and a venerable café where the city's signature drink – the *bicerin* (see page 88) – was invented. In good weather, café tables, an outdoor concert and strolling locals may share the limited space. In the small streets off the piazza are wine bars and shops.

🚇 Via Consolata. 🚌 Bus/tram 3, 16, 52, 60 (note that 52 and 60 stop only westbound).

Santuario di Santa Maria Consolatrice (La Consolata)

Virtually nothing remains in Turin of the period under the Franks, from 773 to 940, except the campanile of the Benedictine church of Sant'Andrea, which was preserved by Guarini when he rebuilt it in 1678 as a sanctuary dedicated to Mary. In 1729, Filippo Juvarra added the oval presbytery; investigate the room to its left to see the collection of ex-votos left by the faithful.

ⓐ Piazza della Consolata. ☎ 011.436.3235. ⏰ Daily 06.30–19.30. Mass: Mon–Sat every half hour 06.30–12.00, Sun every hour 0600–12.00 and 18.15–19.30. Ⓝ Bus/tram 3, 16, 52, 60 (note that nos. 52 and 60 stop only westbound).

Palazzo Falletti di Barolo

Step in to see the central staircase and foyer of this patrician home of a Marchesa. You'll need an appointment to see the rooms of the *piano nobile*, which show the lifestyle of 17th-century Turinese aristrocracy.

ⓐ Via Delle Orfane 7. ☎ 011.436.0311. Ⓦ www.palazzobarolo.it ⏰ Sept–July: Mon and Wed 10.00–12.00 and 15.00–17.00, Fri 10.00–12.00; Aug: Mon, Wed, Fri 10.00–12.00. Admission charged. Ⓝ Bus/tram 3, 16, 52, 60 (note that 52 and 60 stop only westbound).

Via Garibaldi

Leading west from Palazzo Madama, the street was designed in 1775, following the route of the Roman *decimus maximus*. Today it is a pedestrianised kilometre of shops. To meet 75 per cent of Turin's population, go there on a Saturday afternoon.

Ⓝ Bus/tram 4, 11, 11, 12, 27, 50, 51, 57.

Cappella della Pia Congregazione dei Banchieri e dei Mercanti

One of Turin's best-kept secrets, this baroque gem is hidden behind a cloister, Antichi Chiostri. Built in 1692 for the Pious Congregation of Merchants and Bankers and dedicated to the Epiphany, the chapel's highlight is a vaulted ceiling painted in frescoes by Legnanino.

ⓐ Via Garibaldi 25; ☎ 011.562.7226. Ⓝ Bus/tram 4, 11, 11, 12, 27, 50, 51, 57. ⏰ Sat 15.00–18.00, Sun 10.00–12.00, closed July and August. Mass: Sun 11.00.

⬢ *The city's Roman origins are still visible*

Chiesa di San Francesco d'Assisi (Church of St Francis of Assisi)

The original convent church was built in the 1300s, and was once home to the Holy Shroud during 16th-century repairs to the Duomo. In this church, St John Bosco (founder of the Salesian Order, which

rescues and educates abandoned children) celebrated his first mass after his ordination. It was also here that he met the child who inspired his order.

❷ Via San Francesco d'Assisi 11. ☎ 011.562.8474. 🕐 Mon–Sat 07.00–13.00 and 15.30–19.30, Sun 09.00–12.00 and 16.30–20.00. Mass: Mon–Sat 18.45, Sun 19.15. 🚌 Bus/tram 4, 11, 11, 12, 27, 50, 51, 57 (all stop southbound only).

Piazza Solferino

Nineteenth-century buildings surround the piazza, including Palazzo Ceriena and Teatro Alfiera. In its centre, next to a 1930 fountain of the four seasons, is the highly controversial ultra-modern Atrium Torino, built in 2004 to herald the city's transformation for the 2006 Winter Olympics. The future of the wood, glass and steel structure after the Olympics is uncertain, but for the present it serves quite nicely as a tourist information point and display space.

❷ Via Pietra Micca connects this long, busy piazza to Piazza.

Art nouveau buildings

To find *Stile Liberty* (art nouveau, see box on page 82) buildings, wander Corso Francia from Piazza Statudo, looking up to spot curving windows, floral (and sometimes florid) decoration, sweeping reverse curves and asymmetrical forms typical of the style. Some better-known examples are at the corners of Via Principe d'Acaja and Via Bagetti, and at no. 23 Corso Francia. Other streets in the neighbourhood have outstanding examples, too: look for the wrought-iron work on Via Piffetti 3–5 and if you're hooked after this sampler, seek out Casa Florio on via San Francesco d'Assisi 17, Casa Avezzano on Via Giovanni Battista Vico 2 (at Via Andrea

Massena), Casa Sigismondi at Via Madama Cristina 5, and two on Corso Ferraris at nos. 22 and 78. Or, without wandering from the beaten path at all, you can sample the style at Palazzo Bellia, Via Pietro Micca nos. 4–8, between Piazza Solferino and Piazza Castello.

CULTURE

The museums of these two districts are more widely scattered than those around the Palazzo Reale, but the streets between them are so filled with funky shops, wine bars and eye-catching architecture that you won't mind the distances.

Museo di Antichità (Museum of Antiquity)

The Savoys converted the former Orangerie of their palace into a venue for displaying collections of artefacts from all the ancient Italian diaspora, which includes much of the Mediterranean region. Especially good exhibits feature ancient Cyprus and the Etruscans. Amid these, it's easy to overlook finds from the local Piedmont area, but the collections do include material from prehistoric sites and from the elusive Frankish years. Look for the Marengo treasure, discovered in 1928, that includes silver and gold work from the first and second centuries AD.

⊙ Via XX Settembre 88. ⊙ 011.521.1106. ⊙ Tues–Sun 08.30–19.30. Admission charged. ⊙ Bus/tram 13, 56, 57, 63.

Museo della Sindone (Museum of the Holy Shroud)

The crypt of the San Sudario di Torino church is the site of a museum that examines the history, science, religion and art of one of Christendom's most celebrated and controversial relics. Since it's run by a religious confraternity – the Brotherhood of the Holy

THE NEW LOOK

The art nouveau style rocked European art and architecture at the turn of the 20th century, with bold new shapes and designs that shocked the stuffy traditionalists of the art establishment. The new look delighted the rising moneyed class of new industrialists, who were looking for ways to carve their own niche in society – and in Turin. The city had plenty of these entrepreneurs with its new automobile plants springing up, and they wanted to mark their own turf in central Turin, where the old Savoy cronies still held sway. Nothing could have suited this brash crowd of movers and doers better than a fresh and flamboyant look for their houses.

In 1902 the General Exposition in Turin was just the inspiration they needed, as the foremost architects and artists strutted their newest stuff: flowing lines, deep curves, decorated tiles, floral and nature themes all translated into architectural materials. So art nouveau – called *Stile Liberty* in Italy – became the new look for the previously undeveloped areas close to the old centre – Corso Francia (beyond Porta Susa rail station) via Cibrario (the westward continuance of Via Garibaldi), the Crocetta (South of Corso Vittorio Emanuele) and the hillside just across the Po.

Shroud – it's not a place you're likely to find cutting-edge theories debunking its authenticity, but the notion of constantly changing 'virtual frescoes' projected on the vaulting and niches by fifteen projectors could be irresistible even to sceptics.

🅐 Via San Domenico 28. 🕐 011.436.5832. 🆆 www.sindone.it

🕐 Daily 09.00–12.00, 15.00–19.00. Admission charged.
🚍 Bus/tram 3, 16, 52, 60 (note that 52 and 60 stop only westbound).

Museo Storico Nazionale dell'Artigliera (National Historical Museum of Artillery)

The Mastio, where this museum is located, is the only standing remnant of the five-sided fortified citadel that gave this part of town its name. The fortifications did their job, withstanding three sieges by the French between 1640 and 1799 before falling to the more powerful forces of civic expansion in the 1850s. Even before the final siege, the Mastio had been made into an artillery museum in 1731, putting it among the world's oldest museums. If you've visited the collections in the Palazzo Reale, it's less of the same, but it does have some rare large weapons.

🏛 Corso Galileo Ferraris. 📞 011.562.9223. 🕐 Mon–Thur 09.00–16.00, Fri 09.00–13.00. Admission charged. 🚍 Bus/tram 13, 29, 51, 52, 55, 56, 59, 60, 72.

Museo Civico Pietro Micca

The tale of Pietro Micca blowing up the tunnel – and himself in the process – to prevent French attackers from entering via the subterranean passageways under the Citadel is a familiar one to every Piedmont schoolchild. This and the story of the siege of 1706 are recounted here, but the best part is that you can tour the underground tunnels. The model of Turin in the 1700s, when the walls still enclosed this whole part of the city, is interesting, too.

🏛 Via Guicciardini 7. 📞 011.546.317. 🕐 Tues–Sun 09.00–19.00. Tunnel tours half-hourly morning, hourly afternoon. Admission charged.
🚍 Bus/tram 1, 10, 55, 65.

Museo della Marionetta Piemontese

Strung marionettes and hand puppets – thousands of them – along with stages, costumes and other puppetiana have been collected by the Lupi family of puppeteers. Since the 1700s this family has not only presented marrionette theatre, but has worked to keep the traditions alive and fresh. The museum includes a theatre (see page 92) with regular performances.

🅐 Via Santa Teresa 5. 🅣 011.530.238. 🅦 www.marionettelupi.com
🅛 Sept–July: Mon–Fri 09.30–13.00 , 1400–17.00. Admission charged.
🅝 Bus/tram 1, 4, 9, 11, 12, 15, 18, 50, 51, 55, 56, 61, 67, 68 (note that several of these stop only on their north or southbound routes).

Galleria Civica d'Arte Moderna e Contemporanea (GAM) (Modern Art Gallery)

Interesting exhibits compare works of local avant-garde luminaries with their more famous contemporaries. The time period stretches from the 18th to the 21st century and the collections, although primarily Italian, include works by Paul Klee, Max Ernst and others of their note.

🅐 Via Magenta 31. 🅣 011.442.9518. 🅦 www.gamtorino.it 🅛 Tues–Sun 09.00–19.00, free admission all day Tues. 🅝 Bus/tram 1, 64.

RETAIL THERAPY

The little back streets of the Quadrilatero are peppered with small shops; for wearables by young and hopeful designers, head for Via Bonelli, where boutiques feature the newest and funkiest. Via Garibaldi is an almost solid kilometre of shops, and the continent's biggest street market is in Piazza della Repubblica. Choose Via Mercanti for fine craftsmanship – bookbinders, chandlers and handmade paper goods.

Porta Palazzo Europe's largest open-air market sprawls across the piazza and into neighbouring streets, with stalls piled high in fresh produce, meats, cheeses, spices, clothes, cooking pots, dishes and gadgets. On Sunday it morphs into a mind-numbing antiques and second-hand market called Il Balon, which on the second Sunday of each month expands to become Il Gran Balon. The real treasures go early, and bargaining is expected.

ⓐ Piazza della Republica. ⓛ Mon–Fri 07.30–13.00, Sat 07.30–19.30.
ⓝ Bus/tram 3, 15, 19, 50, 51.

🔻 *Porta Palazzo market is just the place for picnic supplies*

Luigi Franco Deep in the Quadrilatero, this art gallery specializes in modern artists in all media – painting, photography, sculpture and more. 🄰 Via Sant'Agostino 23. ☎ 011.521.1336. 🕒 Tues–Sat 16.00–20.00.

Weber A number of contemporary artists began their careers here; look for tomorrow's greats and the latest art trends. 🄰 Via San Tommaso. ☎ 011.812.3519. 🕒 Tues–Sat 16.00–19.30.

Luigi Conterno One of Turin's oldest shops, Conterno has been making fine candles since the late 1700s. You'll find everything from tiny candles for birthday cakes and figurals imitating vegetables to stylish dinner table tapers. 🄰 Piazza Solferino 3. ☎ 011.562.2550. 🚍 Bus/tram 5, 14, 29, 50, 57. No credit cards.

La Casa Moderna Sleek, chic, modern housewares, including the latest bright plastic kitchen toy from the Piedmont's own Alessi. 🄰 Corso Re Umberto 1. 🚍 Bus/tram 5, 14.

Mercantino della Crocetta Can't afford Via Roma? Head here for high fashion at lower prices. 🄰 Largo Cassini (Via Marco Polo). 🕒 Mon–Fri 08.30–13.00, Sat 08.30–18.30.

TAKING A BREAK

Part of the reason for wandering the Quadrilatero is to stop in its little side-street cafés and wine bars – whether you're feeling peckish or your feet just need a break from the pavement. Between

▶ *Turin is a paradise for the sweet toothed*

Via Garibaldi and Via Guilio, every third doorway seems to lead to food and drink. Small plates of snacks and light lunches are best found in these bars and cafés; anything less than a full meal can be hard to find in restaurants. Tiny cafés on the east side of Piazza della Repubblica serve very cheap pizza and other foods midday as the market winds down.

Al Bicerin Choose the drink it's named for – *bicerin*: equal parts espresso, hot chocolate and cream – and enjoy it outside if the weather cooperates. The pastries are excellent. ➋ Piazza della Consolata 5. ➊ 011.436.9325. ➌ www.bicerin.it ➍ closed Wed. ➎ Bus/tram 3, 16, 52, 60 (52 and 60 stop only westbound).

Olsen € Just off Via Garibaldi, this little bakery/café is well known for inexpensive lunches, which accounts for it being full most of the time. Stop by off-hours for the pastry. ➋ Via Sant'Agostino 4. ➊ 011.436 1573.

La Pergola Rosa € Risotto is a specialty here, a filling lunch for a blustery day. Desserts are made in-house. ➋ Via Settembre 18. ➊ 011.537 562. ➍ Closed Sun and Aug.

La Taverna di Guitti € Also just off Via Garibaldi, this taverna serves a plate of starters that is an ample lunch, or order a hearty plate of house-made tagliolini. ➋ Via San Dalmazzo 1. ➊ 011.533.164. ➍ Closed Sat lunch and Sun.

San Tommaso 10 Serious coffee drinkers head here, where the family has been roasting beans for more than a century, to drink flavoured cappuccinos and espressos. ➋ San Tommaso 10. ➊ 011.534.201. ➍ Daily. ➎ Bus/tram 5, 14, 29, 50, 59, 67.

Confetteria Chocolate and coffee go hand in hand here – or rather spoon in cup, since the coffee spoons are chocolate coated. ⓐ Via San Francesco d'Assisi 17. ⓛ Daily. ⓝ Bus/tram 4, 12, 27, 50, 51, 57.

Amici Miei Pizza and focaccio are served in an unfancy setting near the modern art museum (GAM – see page 84). ⓐ Corso Vittorio Emanuele 94. ⓣ 011.506.9961. ⓛ Daily, Sat–Sun evening meal only. ⓝ Bus/tram 9, 68.

AFTER DARK

The Quadrilatero's side-street wine bars and *trattorie* begin to get lively at about 19.00, as the Turinese drift in for their evening ritual – the *aperitivo*. Plates of small bites and starters appear on tables with the drinks, and for many locals, replace dinner entirely. Music, occasionally live, goes with the food and drink To really fit in, move from one to the next, sampling the food at each. North of these streets is the city's hottest new late-night scene, Docks Dora, in the old warehouses near the Dora River.

Restaurants

Brek Ristoranti € A quick glance through the glass wall tells you this place is different: fresh fruit and vegetables are everywhere, and the entire kitchen is visible. Take a tray and select your own meal – cooked before your eyes – and pay according to serving size. ⓐ Piazza Solferino. ⓣ 011.545.424. ⓝ Bus/tram 5, 14, 29, 50, 57.

La Campana € Trendy dishes, such as *bresaola* with *arugola*, along with the traditional local favourites of *agnolotti* (a meat-filled ravioli) and braised beef in Barolo wine are on the menu at this

restaurant near the Duomo. ❸ Via XX Settembre 79. ❶ 011.521.4011.
Ⓦ www.hotelchelsea.it Ⓛ Closed Sun and two weeks in Aug.
Ⓝ Bus/tram 4, 11, 11, 12, 27, 50, 51, 57 (all stop northbound only).

Solferino € The chef is fanatic about using fresh locally-grown
ingredients to prepare Tuscan dishes as well as Piedmont
specialties. ❸ Piazza Solferino 3. ❶ 011.535.851. Ⓝ Bus/tram 5, 14, 29,
50, 57.

Antica Bruschetteria Pautasso €–€€ Full of local character, this
homey restaurant serves a good *bagna cauda* – vegetables with a
rich dipping sauce of cream, garlic and anchovies. ❸ Piazza E.
Filliberto 4. ❶ 011.436.6706. Ⓝ Bus/tram 3, 16 (closest stop is at the
west end of Piazza della Republica).

Il Lanternin €€ Try the veal cutlet with vegetables, a specialty of the
Val d'Aosta region, or the house specialty pasta, *tagliolini*. ❸Via della
Consolata 1. ❶ 011.562.5311. Ⓛ Closed Sun and all of Aug. Ⓝ Bus/tram
3, 16, 52, 60 (note that 52 and 60 stop only westbound).

Osteria Arcano Matto €€ The location for a wine bar/restaurant
doesn't get any better, halfway between piazzas Solferino and Castello.
The menu is upmarket and innovative, but not overpriced; look for the
daily special. ❸ Via Pietro Micca 17. ❶ 011.547.953. Ⓦ www.arcanomatto.
com Ⓝ Bus/tram 5, 14, 29, 50, 57 or any for Piazza Castello.

Vintage 1997 €€–€€€ Contemporary atmosphere and a chance to

---

❿ *A cocktail and some appetisers is a good way to begin the evening in the
Quadrilatero*

sample dishes from Italy's various regions make this a good respite from the same-old. As you can guess from the name, the wine list is extensive. ➌ Piazza Solferino 16/h. ➊ 011.535.948. ➌ Closed Sun and all of Aug. Ⓝ Bus/tram 5, 14, 29, 50, 57.

Cinemas & theatres

Teatro Alfieri One of Italy's best-known theatres, the Alfieri stages major plays and comedies. In new space are two additional theatres for cinema, showing mostly art films. ➌ Piazza Solferino 4. ➊ 011.562.3800. Ⓦ www.torinospettacoli.it Ⓝ Bus/tram 5, 14, 29, 50, 57.

Teatro Juvarra Dedicated to avante garde theatre, the Juvarra is known for multi-media, new technologies and experimental productions. ➌ Via Juvarra 15. Near Piazza Statuto, a major bus/tram hub. ➊ 011.540.675. Ⓦ www.juvarramultiteatro.it

Café Procope Under the theatre, the café stages its own shows and concerts, as well as being a pleasant place for a drink. ➌ Via Juvarra 15. ➊ 011.540.675. Ⓦ www.juvarramultiteatro.it

Teatro Gianduja The tiny theatre, part of the marionette museum, is where the puppets perform. Productions include those for children, but most are for all ages. ➌ Via Santa Teresa 5. ➊ 011.530.238. Ⓦ www.marionettelupi.com Ⓝ Bus/tram 1, 4, 9, 11, 12, 15, 18, 50, 51, 55, 56, 61, 67, 68 (note that several of these stop only on their north- or southbound routes).

Clubs, bars & discos

L'Albero di Vino In a lively little square at the edge of the Quadrilatero, this is a good stop before hitting the late-night spots

at Docks Dora. ⓐ Piazza della Consolata 9. ⓛ Daily 19.00–01.00.
ⓝ Bus/tram 3, 16, 52, 60 (note that 52 and 60 stop only westbound).

Arancia di Mezzanotte Instead of the usual plate of snacks on the
table, this trendy spot serves a buffet with your apertif.
ⓐ Piazza E. Filibert 11. ⓛ Open 18.00–01.00. ⓝ Bus/tram 3, 16 (closest
stop is at the west end of Piazza della Republica).

Teatro The cavernous former theatre (hence the name) is divided
into three floors of high-tech architecture, with the dance floor on
the former stage. ⓐ Via Sta Teresa 10 (near Via Roma). ⓣ 011.518.7107.
ⓛ Tues–Sun 20.00–02.00. ⓝ Bus/tram 1, 4, 9, 11, 12, 15, 18, 50, 51, 55, 56,
61, 67, 68 (note that several of these stop only on their north- or
southbound routes).

Ambhara Bar Among the first bars to open in the Docks Dora area,
Ambhara attracts a smart clientele with a fusion menu, cocktails,
aperitifs and an especially good regional wine list. ⓐ Via Borgo Dora
10. ⓣ 011.521.7346. ⓛ 19.00–02.00.

Officine Belforte At the Docks Dora, Xplosiva DJs spin acid techno
and dark groove on Fri; Sat is hip hop and R&B. Another Docks Dora
legend-in-the-making, **Docks8** has two levels with techno and
electro accompanied by videos. Stay on for the Scatafashion – the
Sunday morning hold-over scene. ⓐ Corso Venizia 30. ⓣ 011.819.4347.
ⓦ www.barumba.com ⓛ Fri–Sat 24.00–06.00. Closed July–Aug.

Folkclub West of the Quadrilatero (and too late for the buses) the taxi
ride is worth it for world music and jazz, often with international
artists. ⓐ Via Perrone 3b. ⓣ 011.537.636. ⓦ www.folkclub.it (Italian).

Along the Po

The River Po tiptoes softly past Turin, a lazy waterway for paddle and sightseeing boats, spanned by graceful bridges and lined by grassy parkland and waterside restaurants. Via Po, which sweeps grandly from the Palazzo Reale complex, ends just as dramatically at the river, in Piazza Vittoria Veneto. The habitués of the cafés under its porticoes are university students and expats. The river's opposite bank rises into the rarified atmosphere of Borgo Po, its art nouveau villas half hidden in their private parks. Above a pair of churches offer views of the city from their terraces.

SIGHTS & ATTRACTIONS

If the Savoy centre is characterised by its baroque palaces and the Quadrilatero by its architectural diversity, the neighbourhoods along the Po claim the city's top architectural surprises. Make that oddities. The Mole rises head and shoulders above the city like a spiked army helmet, bars and clubs hide under street support arches by the river, a faux medieval village springs from the riverbank and a posh restaurant perches on a rooftop auto test track.

Mole Antonelliana

Symbol of the city, and its best viewpoint if you've a head for heights, the Mole's history is as strange as its architecture. Its name translates to Antonelli's Heap, for Alessandro Antonelli, its architect. It began life as a synagogue, or at least it was intended as one. But it became such an expensive project that the congregation abandoned it to the city, which converted its purpose to a

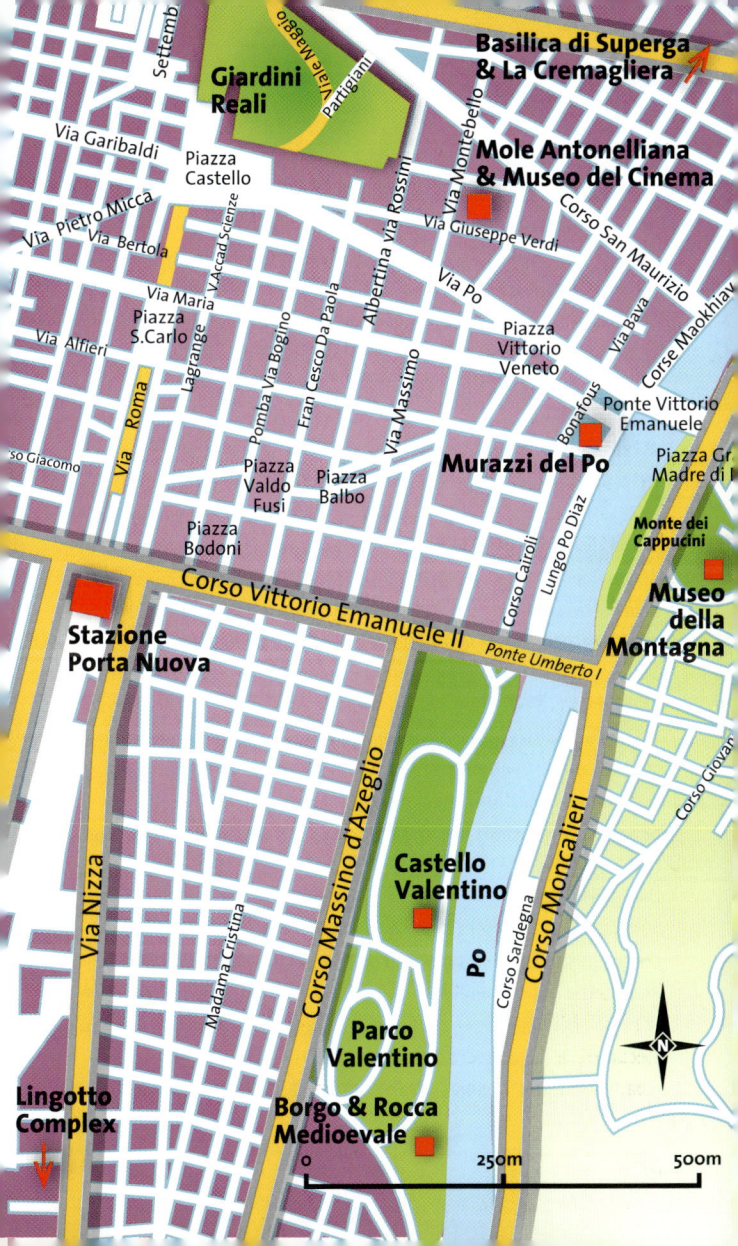

Basilica di Superga & La Cremagliera

Giardini Reali

Mole Antonelliana & Museo del Cinema

Settemb

Viale Maggio

Viale Partigiani

Via Garibaldi

Piazza Castello

Via Montebello

Via Rossini

Corso San Maurizio

Via Pietro Micca

Via Bertola

V.Acad Scienze

Albertina

Via Giuseppe Verdi

Via Maria

Lagrange

Via Po

Via Bava

Corse Maokhiav

Via Alfieri

Piazza S.Carlo

Pomba

Via Bogino

Fran Cesco Da Paola

Piazza Vittorio Veneto

Via Roma

Via Massimo

Bonafous

Ponte Vittorio Emanuele

so Giacomo

Piazza Valdo Fusi

Piazza Balbo

Via Cairoli

Murazzi del Po

Piazza Gr Madre di I

Piazza Bodoni

Corso Cairoli

Lungo Po Diaz

Monte dei Cappucini

Corso Vittorio Emanuele II

Museo della Montagna

Stazione Porta Nuova

Ponte Umberto I

Via Nizza

Corso Massino d'Azeglio

Madama Cristina

Castello Valentino

Po

Corso Sardegna

Corso Moncalieri

Corso Giovan

Parco Valentino

Lingotto Complex

Borgo & Rocca Medioevale

0   250m   500m

N

monument to King Vittorio Emanuele II. But the building itself never had a permanent use until it finally became the site of the Museum of Cinema (see Culture, page 103), a fitting use for this larger-than-life heap. Take the glass lift to the top on a clear day for a breathtaking view of the Alps, and of the city.

ⓐ Via Montebello 20. ⓣ 011.812.5658. ⓛ Tues–Fri 10.00–20.00, Sat 10.00–23.00, Sun 10.00–20.00. Admission charge. ⓝ Bus/tram 13, 15, 16, 55, 56, 61, 68.

Piazza Vittorio Veneto

On reaching the river, arcaded Via Po ends in a flourish. Piazza Vittorio Veneto's impressive size and portico-surrounded perimeter are so perfectly designed that they disguise the 12 m (35ft) difference in street level from one side to the other. In the winter, cafés and restaurants hide under the arcades; in summer they overflow into the pedestrianised areas.

I Murazzi

The 19th-century architects that designed the sturdy arches to support the streets among the Po embankment might be surprised to see them on a summer Saturday night. Under the arcade between Ponto Umberto and Ponto Vittorio Emanuele it's one long block party, as revelers drift from bar to bar to club. In colder seasons the action moves elsewhere, but in summer this is the place to be.

Chiesa di San Massimo (Church of St Maximus)

Built in the 1840s, when this section of the city was being developed, the neo-classical church is of particular interest to musicians, who will want to see and hear the organ. Built by one of the most prominent organ-makers of his day, Carlo Bossi, this enormous

instrument of more than 3000 pipes won the gold medal at the 1884 Italian Exposition, and was a favorite of both Berlioz and Mendelssohn. In the baptistery, Legnanino's 1707 altarpiece depicting the Nativity of the Virgin predates the church by more than a century; the striking large stained-glass window was created in 1949.
🅐 Via Mazzini 29 (corner of Via Massimo, Via Mazzini).
🅣 011.812.6703. 🅛 Mon–Sat 08.00–12.00 and 16.00–19.30, Sun 08.00–12.30 and 17.45–19.30. Mass: Mon–Sat 18.30, Sun 08.30, 10.30, 11.30, 18.30.

Parco Valentino

The green band of parkland stretches for nearly a mile along the Po from Ponte Umberto to Ponte Isabella, much of it facing a green space on the opposite bank and giving the river a rural look in the midst of the city. Vehicle-free Viale Virgilio runs near the river the entire length of the park, a favourite place for walkers, cyclists and joggers in the daytime. It leads to sites within the park, an excursion boat landing and several waterside restaurants.
🅐 Corso Vittorio Emanuele, Corso Massimo D'Azeglio. 🅝 Bus/tram 9, 16, 52.

Castello Valentino

Bought by the Savoys in 1564, not long after it was built, it served as a residence until it became home to the university's Department of Architecture. Although it's officially not open to the public, you can usually just walk in and look around. 🅐 Parco Valentino, Corso Massimo D'Azeglio. 🅝 Bus/tram 9, 16, 52.

Orto Botanico (Botanic Gardens)

Begun as a source of medicinal plants, this small garden contains rare and alpine plants and a herbarium. ❷ Parco Valentino, Corso Massimo D'Azeglio.❶ 011.661.2447. ❸ Sat–Sun 09.00–13.00, 15.00–19.00. Admission charge. ❷ Bus/tram 9, 16, 52.

Borgo Medioevale

Whenever someone who has never been to Turin suggests that it's a grim industrial city, tell them about Borgo Medioevale – living proof that Turin is a city with a sense of humour. This enclave of shops and public buildings appears to be a somewhat over-restored part of the medieval city, but in fact it was built about 400 years too late. Carefully constructed using old techniques and replicating existing architecture and decoration of the period from the surrounding region, the whole village was part of the 1884 Exposition. Entrance is free, and inside are shops, craftsmen (including an armour repair shop in case yours is dented) and buildings to wander among.
❷ Viale Virgilio, Parco Valentino, Corso Massimo D'Azeglio.
❶ 011.433.1701. ❸ Apr–Oct Daily 09.00–20.00, Nov–Mar Daily 9.00–19.00. Admission free. ❷ Bus/tram 9, 16, 52.

Rocca Medioevale

Also built for the Exposition, the castle is a convincing replica of those that line the Val d'Aosta, including frescoes faithfully copied from them. A modest admission is charged for a tour of the building, which even has period sound effects.
❷ Viale Virgilio, Parco Valentino, Corso Massimo D'Azeglio.
❶ 011.433.1701. ❸ Tues–Sun 09.00–19.00. Admission charge.
❷ Bus/tram 9, 16, 52.

---

❶ *Turin's most striking building, the Mole Antonelliana*

Valentina & Valentino

Modern glass-enclosed boats cruise from the Borgo Medioevale downstream to the Murazzo or upstream as far as Moncalieri, for views of the city and river landscapes.

🅐 Parco Valentino, Corso Massimo D'Azeglio. Operated by GTT. 🅣 011.546.4733, reservations 011.744.892. 🅦 www.gtt.to.it 🅛 Departing Nov–Apr Sun only, May and Oct Sun and holidays, June–Sept Tues–Sun, 15.00,1615 (by reservation only) and 17.45. July –Sept also at 19.00, 2130, 22.45 (last two trips by reservation only). 🅝 Bus/tram 13, 15, 16, 30, 53, 55, 56, 61, 70.

Lingotto Complex

Renzo Piano was commissioned to transform Fiat's first American-style assembly line plant, built 1923, into a showpiece and he succeeded. Bold designs and state-of-the-art techno features – window blinds that follow the sun, glass roofs that slide into place over courtyard cafés in case of rain – turned the redundant factory into 90 shops, two hotels, an art museum and a rooftop restaurant you can drive to. The rooftop test track with Alpine views is now a running and walking track for hotel guests. Fiat enthusiasts should stop to see the first Fiat factory at 102 Corso Dante, just past Parco Valentino, a 1904–06 *Stile Liberty* (art nouveau) building designed by Alfredo Premoli.

🅐 Via Nizza 280. 🅛 Otto Gallery (shopping) Mon 12.00–22.00, Tues–Sun 10.00–22.00. Admission free. 🅝 Bus/tram 1, 18, 35.

Chiesa dei Gran Madre di Dio (Church of the Mother of God)

Built in thanksgiving for the return of the Savoys from exile during the Napoleonic occupation, the church is modelled on Rome's Pantheon. Rumours suggesting that the Holy Grail is hidden here are probably exaggerated.

🔺 *Plenty of places to eat and drink along the lazy River Po*

ⓐ Piazza Gran Madre. ⓣ 011.819.3572. ⓛ Mon–Sat 07.30–12.00 and 16.30–19.00, Sun 07.30–13.00, 15.30–19.00, 20.30–22.00 (Aug 07.30–12.00, 16.00–19.00. Mass: Mon–Sat 08.00, 09.00, 18.30, Sun 08.30, 10.00, 11.00, 12.00, 18.00, 21.00 (Aug Mon–Fri 08.00, 18.30, Sat 18.00. ⓥ Bus/tram 13, 55, 56, 61.

Chiesa di Santa Maria del Monte

Capuchin friars still occupy the convent for which this church was built in the early 1600s. Its height provides it with a view, but nothing to match that from the Museo della Montagna, farther up (see page 104).

ⓐ Via Giardino 35. ⓣ 011.660.4414. ⓛ Daily 0830–12.00, 15.00–1930; Mass Mon–Sat 1830, Sun 11.00 and 17.00. ⓝ Bus 53. Torino Card (see page 52) holders can take the tourist bus here.

Basilica di Superga

Built as a votive offering following the city's deliverance from the 1706 siege by the French, the church is considered architect Filippo Juvarra's masterpiece. Below (the stairs are to the left of the entrance) are the Savoy tombs and off the cloister is a memorial to the Turinese football team killed in a plane crash here in 1949.
ⓐ Strada della Basilica di Superga 73. ⓣ 011.898.0083. ⓛ Oct–Mar Daily 09.00–12.00 and 15.00–17.00; Apr–Sept 09.00–12.00, 15.00–18.00. Mass: Mon–Sat 10.00, Sun 10.00, 11.00, 12.00, 17.00, Oct–Mar; 10.00, 11.00, 12.00, 18.00 Apr–Sept . ⓝ Bus/tram 15, 61 to the Sassi-Superga Railway (La Cremagliera).

La Cremagliera

Use the rack railway to access the basilica or the walking trails that weave through the natural park at the top, or just for the ride and the views of Turin and the Alps.
ⓐ Sassi. ⓛ Mon, Wed–Fri 09.00–12.00, 14.00–20.00, Tues 19.00–24.00, Sat–Sun 9.00–20.00, leaving Sassi on the hour and Superga on the half hour. ⓝ Bus/tram 15, 60.

CULTURE

Although this part of Turin is not as packed with museums as the area around the Savoy palace, it has its fair share, including the cinema museum and one of Europe's best collections of classic and antique cars.

Museo Nazionale del Cinema

Beginning with the earliest work of the Lumière brothers, this state-of-the-art spectacle dazzles with themed exhibits on various genre, the technical process, sets, personalities, film stars and every other facet of the industry. Watch film classics in a variety of theatre settings, including a heart-shaped bed (for love stories, of course). Props, sets and stage models round out an experience that will please any film fan.

🚊 Via Montebello 20. ☎ 011.812.5658. 🌐 www.museonazionale delcinema.org 🕐 Tues–Fri 10.00–20.00, Sat 10.00–23.00, Sun 10.00–20.00. Admission charge. 🚌 Bus/tram 13, 15, 16, 55, 56, 61, 68.

Museo di Arti Decorative

Silver, paintings, porcelain, tapestries, furniture and various *objets d'art* celebrate the decorative skills of 18th-century artists and craftsmen. The museum is based on the private collections of the legendary Turin antique dealer, Pietro Accorsi, who left them – and a legacy for the museum – to the city. Tours are provided in English.

🚊 Via Po 55. ☎ 011.812.9116. 🌐 www.fondazioneaccorsi.it 🕐 Tues–Wed, Fri, Sun 10.00–23.00, Thur 10.00–20.00. Admission charge. 🚌 Bus/tram 13, 15, 16, 30, 61, 55, 56.

Museo dell'Automobile (Motor Museum)

The collection of about 170 vehicles is one of the largest in the world, and ensconced in a 1960s building that is a splendid example of modern architecture. The cars date from the very earliest motor vehicles, designed and built in the mid-1800s. Italian makes predominate the collections, with an even dozen Alfa Romeos, eight Ferraris, 27 Fiats (this is their home, after all), three Maseratis, four Isotta Fraschinis and a couple of Bugatis. But other significant

makes and places are represented too, with cars from France, Great Britain, Germany, Holland, Spain, Poland and the United States and including such makes as Packard, Mercedes Benz, Rolls-Royce, Jaguar and Stanley Steamer. Along with road models are racing cars and rare examples of celebrity cars used in movies.

ⓐ Corso Unità d'Italia 40. ❶ 011.677.666. Ⓦ www.museoauto.it
🕐 Tues–Sun 10.00–18.30. Admission charge.
Ⓝ Bus/tram 1, 18, 34, 35, 45, 74.

Pinacoteca Giovanni e Marella Agnelli

The selections from Giovanni e Marella Agnelli's art collection – one of Italy's most significant and of which this is but a small fraction – are shown in a purpose-built gallery designed by Renzo Piano. The Turinese call it *lo scrigno* (the casket) for its peculiar shape, appended onto the Lingotto. The few (about two dozen) works shown include some outstanding ones, by by Tiepolo, Manet, Renoir, Matisse and Modigliani, along with six Venetian scenes by Canaletto.

ⓐ Via Nizza 230. ❶ 011.006.2713. 🕐 Tues–Sun 09.00–19.00.
Admission charge. Ⓝ Bus/tram 1, 18, 35.

Museo Nazionale della Montagna (Mountain Museum)

Exhibits in this surprisingly complete museum include mountain traditions, art, geology, natural history, alpine plants and wildlife, as well as the development of mountaineering sports (both climbing and skiing), in the Alps and other ranges where sport climbing is popular. Interesting as this may be, if the day is clear, many people give these exhibits short notice on their way to the observation level. Here the Alps themselves spread before you in a magnificent panorama, well worth the climb up the Capuchins' mountain.

ⓐ Via Giadino 39 – Monte dei Cappuccini.

🕓 011.660.4104. 🌐 www.museomontagna.org 🕐 Tues–Sun
09.00–19.00. Admission charge. 🚍 Bus 53

RETAIL THERAPY

Between the pricey big-name shops of the Via Roma and the equally
pricey boutiques of the Borgo Po is the University, bringing reason to
the prices, but wild abandon to the styles. Shop under the arcades of
Via Po for funky clothes (and second-hand books in all languages)
and along trendy (and correspondingly more expensive) Via Mazziniʳ
for higher fashion, sometimes off-price from designers.

Dobhran Clothing and accessories for men and women mix with
books published by the Slow Foods movement in this upmarket
shop. 🚏 Via San Massimo 53. 🕓 011.88.351. 🌐 www.dobhran.it
🚍 Bus/tram 9, 18, 52.

Gioielli da Calzare If clothes can be radical and classic all at once,
this shop does it with the kind of shoes and accessories that chic Via
Mazzini shoppers expect. 🚏 Via Mazzini, 7/F (at Carlo Alberto).
🕓 011.546.592. 🚍 Bus/tram 49, 15, 63.

Scout Maybe tries just a little too hard to be on the cutting edge of
la bella figura, but a good place to stay ahead of the pack.
🚏 Via Mazzini 1. 🕓 011.533.000. 🕐 Bus/tram 9, 13, 15, 18, 52, 56, 61,
67, 68

Creativity Housewares and whatevers, from top designers and
emerging craftsmen, all share the originality of their design to be
shown here. 🚏 Via Mazzini 29. 🕓 011.817.7864. 🕐 Bus/tram 18, 61, 68.

Giulebbe Pack an elegant picnic here and head for the riverbank at Parque Valentino. No bargains, but top quality food gifts from the length of Italy. ➋ Via della Rocca 39 (just off Via Mazinni). ➊ 011.882.55. ➌ Bus/tram 16, 52.

Maze Lively venue to see the work of young artists without the pomp of the more establishment galleries. ➋ Via Mazzini 40. ➊ 011.815.4145. ➌ Longer hours than most traditional galleries: Mon–Fri 10.30am–19.30, Sat 15.00–20.00.

TAKING A BREAK

The arcades of Piazza Victoria Veneto and Via Po scarcely conceal the multitude of cafés that provide a second home to university students. Other small cafés scatter along the streets near the Po, so you're never far from a place for an espresso or a Negroni.

Caffe Elena Students mix with literary types in this classic café that was a favorite of Nietzsche. It's one of the many that spill out into the piazza in good weather. This historical café is located in the small pedestrian zone facing Piazza Vittoria. ➋ Piazza Vittorio Veneto 5. ➊ 011.812.3341. ➌ Closed Wed. ➍ Bus/tram 13, 15, 16, 30, 53, 55, 61.

La Drogheria Go for an apertif in the late afternoon or for lunch. The apertif hour is a sacred institution here, accompanied by tasty snacks that a fashionable youngish set stops in for every afternoon. ➋ Piazza Vittorio Veneto 18. ➊ 011.812.2414. ➌ Closed Wed. ➍ Bus/tram 13, 15, 16, 30, 53, 55, 61.

▶ *Not as old as it might appear – the Borgo Medioevale*

Cremeria Ghigo Famous since the Savoys nibbled their Ghigo chocolates, this is a busy place from breakfast into the tiny hours. The speciality is anything cream-filled or cream-topped. ⓐ Via Po 52. ⓣ 011.887.017. ⓛ 07.30–20.00 Mon–Sat, 07.30–13.30 Sun. ⓝ Bus/tram 13, 15, 16, 30, 53, 55, 61.

Vinicola Al Sorji Apertifs, an excellent wine list and a few well-prepared meal options make this wine bar a few steps from Piazza Vittorio Veneto popular. ⓐ Via Matteo Pescatore 10. ⓣ 011.835.667. ⓦ www.alsorij.it ⓛ 18.00–12.00 Mon–Sat. ⓝ Bus/tram 13, 15, 16, 30, 53, 55, 61.

Silvano A little bit tatty at the edges and a little bit out of the way – unless you are visiting the Lingotto building – but worth the trip for what many insist are Turin's best fruit *gelati*. ⓐ Via Nizza 142. ⓣ 011.696.0647. Closed Mon. ⓝ Bus/tram 1, 18, 35.

Cantine Risso Lunches are excellent, especially the salads in the summer. Sample local wines in their wine bar in the evening. Corso Casale runs along the opposite side of the Po. ⓐ Corso Casale 79. ⓣ 011.819.5531. ⓛ Closed all day Sat and Sun lunch. ⓝ Bus/tram 13, 51, 61.

AFTER DARK

The evening begins with an *aperitivo* or two in the cafés of Piazza Vittorio Veneto (where you might meet Subsonica in Caffe Elena – their studio is just around the corner). The late-night buzz increases as you move toward the river, reaching a crescendo under the arches built to support the riverside streets. The Murazzi opens onto the river itself and it is the summer meeting point for late clubbers, who jump from one place to another, and for those who just enjoy the music beat from the outside. The only things outnumbering the glasses of wine consumed here on a summer evening are the mosquitoes, so wear insect repellant with your Euro-casual gear.

Restaurants

AL 24 €–€€ Near the Mole Antonelliana, this small eatery mixes Tuscan influences into its Piemontese cuisine. Look for truffle specials in season. ⓐ Via Montebello 24. ⓣ 011.812.2981. ⓛ Daily, except lunch Mon–Tues. Closed late June–mid-July.

Dai Saletta €–€€ A short walk from Parco Valentino, this small neighbourhood favourite serves local dishes with updated touches. Look for *trifulin* (truffle ravioli) and *arrosto alla crema di nocciole* (roasted veal in a hazelnut cream sauce).
ⓐ Via Belfiore 37. ⓣ 011.668.7867. ⓛ Mon–Sat.
ⓝ Bus/tram 9, 16, 52.

E Sotto la Mole €–€€ Piedmont meets the rest of Italy in the kitchen underneath the Mole Antonelliana. The dining room is lively, the food tasty, plentiful and well-priced. ⓛ Via Montebello 9.
ⓣ 011.817.9398. ⓛ evenings Thur–Tues. ⓝ Bus/tram 13, 15, 16, 55, 56, 61, 68.

Gaia Scienza €–€€ Piedmont traditions mix with a few inventive dishes in this cosy osteria. Along with the expected *bagna cauda* and *fritto misto piemontese* (with meat) is the pasta specialty, penne with gorgonzola and *noci* (filberts). ⓐ Via Guastalla 22 (between Corso Regina and Corso San Maurizio). ⓣ 011.812.3821. ⓛ Mon–Sat.
ⓝ Bus/tram 13, 15, 16, 55, 56, 61, 68.

Idrovolante €€ The waterside setting within a leafy park is enough reason to eat here, but the menu trumps that with dishes such as grilled swordfish with sundried tomatoes and capers or grilled veal with Tallegio, asparagus and fresh marjoram. Traditional country dinner on Sun. ⓐ Viale Virgilio 105, Parco Valentino. ❶ 011.668.7602. ⓦ www.ristoranteidrovolante.com ⓝ Bus/tram 9, 16, 52.

San Giorgio 1884 €€–€€€ While you might expect this restaurant in its mock-medieval setting to be really touristy, it is not, but the menu is more international than most in the city. Occasional live music. ⓐ Viale Millo 6. ❶ 011.669.2131. ⓛ evenings. ⓝ Bus/tram 9, 16, 52.

La Pista €€€ The one reason for driving a car in the city would be to arrive at this rooftop restaurant in the Lingotto building by driving up the spiral ramp to the top. The food and service are top-level, too. ⓐ Lingotto Building, Via Nizza 280. ❶ 011.631.3523. ⓛ 12.30–15.00, 19.30–23.00 Wed–Mon. ⓝ Bus/tram 1, 18, 35.

Theatres & music

Auditorium Giovanni Agnelli Classical performances, particularly chamber music, is the special province of this companion to the Agnelli family's art gallery, in the same complex. ⓐ Via Nizza 280, Lingotto. ❶ 011.664.0458. ⓝ Bus/tram 1, 18, 35.

Teatro Colosseo Toast the annual showing of the *Rocky Horror Show* at this eclectic theatre, which also features popular musicals, stage plays and stand-up routines. ⓐ Via Madama Cristina 71. ❶ 01.669.8034. ⓦ www.teatrocolosseo.it

---

ⓞ *Even the Museum of Cinema has an atmospheric bar*

Clubs, bars & discos

CSA Murazzi Really a community centre, CSA hosts the best regional and Italian alternative bands in a minimalist setting along the river. ⓐ Murazzi del Po, 25; ⓣ 011.835.478. ⓛ 19.00–02.00 Mon–Sat. ⓦ Bus/tram 13, 15, 16, 30, 53, 55, 61.

The Beach Tempo and decibels increase as the night progresses to dance music, from 24.00. Complimentary snack buffet 19.00–21.00 with drinks. ⓐ Murazzi del Po 18. ⓣ 011.888.777. ⓦ www.thebeachtorino.it ⓛ 19.00–04.00 (and for lunch in summer). ⓦ Bus/tram 13, 15, 16, 30, 53, 55, 61.

Centralino Club Live rock and DJ sounds fill the underground venue favoured by a very young crowd; Fri is gay night. ⓐ Via delle Rosine, 16. ⓣ 011.837.500. ⓛ 24.00–05.00 Tues, Thur, 24.00–06.00 Fri–Sun. Closed July–Aug. Admission charge. Bus/tram 13, 15, 55, 61.

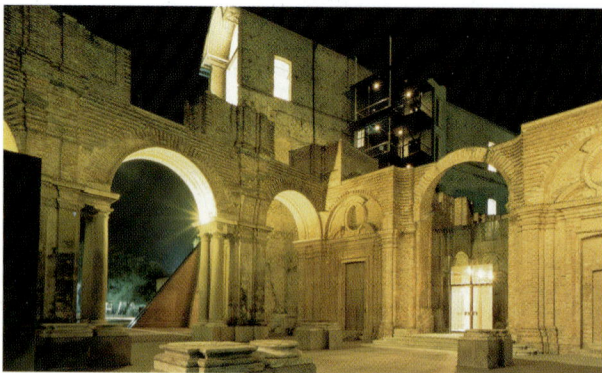

▲ *Castello di Rivolli showing off its magnificence by night*

ROYAL PALACES

Within a short bus ride of the city centre, several of the Savoy royal palaces are open to tour. All are included in the Torino Card (see page 52)

Castello di Rivolli

Duke Emanuele Filiberto first turned this castle into a royal residence. Destroyed by fire by French troops in 1693, it was restored under the architects Michelangelo Garove and Filippo Juvarra, only to fall into disuse after the Napoleonic era. Recent renovations have restored much of its 18th-century magnificence, while creating the Museo d'Arte Contemporanea, which it now houses.

📍 Piazza Malfada di Savoia, Rivoli. 13 km (8 miles) west of Turin. 📞 011.956.522. 🌐 www.castellodirivoli.org . 🕐 10.00–17.00 Tues–Thur, 10.00–21.00 Fri–Sun. Admission charged. 🚌 Bus 36, frequent shuttle weekends from Piazza Castello.

Palazzina di Caccia di Stupinigi

This magnificent baroque palace was begun in 1729 on orders of Carlo Amadeo II and under the direction of Filippo Juvarra. The heavily ornamented rooms were once occupied by Napoleon. It is home to the Museum of Furniture, and extraordinary gardens, also open to the public, fill its surrounding walls.

📍 Piazza Principe Amadeo 7, Stupingi. 📞 011.358.1220. 🌐 www.mauriziano.it/arte/frsetpatr.htm. 🕐 Tues–Sun 10.00–17.00. 🚌 Bus 41.

ROYAL PALACES (continued)

Castello della Mandria and Parco Regionale La Mandria

The castle is actually a collection of 25 structures that belonged to the Savoy kings. The apartments of Borgo Castello, the principal royal residence, can be seen on a guided tour. On the park grounds are old farmsteads, such as the Cascina Comba and the Cascina Vittoria. Look for the chapel of San Giuliano, which dates from 1263. Bicycling and horse riding are available here.

ⓐ Via Carlo Emanuele II 256, Veneria Reale. **ⓣ** 011.499.3311. **ⓦ** www.parks.it/parco.mandria. **ⓛ** Daily 08.00–20.00 Mar–Sept, earlier closing rest of the year. **ⓝ** Bus 72 from Piazza Castello to Venaria (Ponte Vedre entrance is 2.5km from stop).

Reggia di Venaria Reale

Begun in 1659 as a palace with supporting village, its size is often compared to Versailles. The great architects Castellmonte, Garove, Juvarra and Alfiere all contributed to its design and construction. Long neglected, it is in the process of restoration.

ⓐ Piazza della Republica 4, Venaria Reale. **ⓣ** 011.562.3530. **ⓦ** www.reggiavenariareale.it/visite. **ⓛ** Tues, Thurs, Sat–Sun and holidays 09.00–11.30, 14.30–19.00. **ⓝ** Buses 72, 77 to Venaria Reale.

ⓓ *Head out of town and get your skis on*

The Olympic mountain towns

Until 2006, the Val di Susa, Val del Chisone and neighbouring valleys were ski and summer sports havens known to very few beyond Turin and Milan. The announcement that Turin and these valleys would host the 2006 Winter Games changed all that. What did not change is the spectacular scenery or the basic feel of these little villages, where high-style ski wear and late-night discos blend with wilderness trails and centuries-old mountain traditions.

SIGHTS & ATTRACTIONS

Along with the skiing and multiple other winter sports, this region offers summer hiking, mountain biking and alpine rides. A knock-out fortress monastery and some Roman sites add to the mix, but the scenery alone is worth hiring a car or hopping on the direct train into the mountains. Access these valleys on the A32 or the slower S25. To get to the A32 from downtown Turin, follow Corso Regine Margarite.

Sacra di San Michele

The towering monastery dominates its surroundings from the top of Mount Pirchiriano. Begun in 983, it was the home to a powerful Benedictine community until it was closed in 1622. While parts of the complex are in ruins, major portions have been restored. Particularly impressive are the overpowering entrance facade, the archways at the entrance to the church and the Grand Staircase of the Dead. At the top is an archway carved in the 12th century by Master Nicolao, showing the zodiac and constellations.

ⓐ Via Alla Sacra 14, Sant Ambrogio (near Avigliana).

ⓣ 011.939.130. ⓦ www.sacradisanmichele.com

ITALIA

N

Torino

Avigliana

A32

Sacra di S. Michele

Pinerolo

V a l   d e l   C h i s o n e

V a l   d i   S u s a

Susa

Exilles

Pragelato

Sestriere

Sauze di Cesana

20km

10km

0

FRANCE

Modane

Tunnel de Fréjus

Mt Jafferau

Sauze d'Oulx

Bardonecchia

Melezet   Oulx

Cesana Torinese

🕐 Mon–Fri 09.30–12.30, 15.00–18.00, Sun and holidays 09.30–12.00, 14.40–18.30 (mid-Mar–mid-Oct) Mon–Fri 09.30–12.30, 15.00–17.00, Sun and holidays; 09.30–12.00, 14.40–17.00 (mid-Oct–mid-Mar).

Susa

The Romans may have left Susa in the 4th century AD, but their buildings far outlasted them. Look for the massive gateway, Porta Savoia, built in the 2nd century AD. Both ends are embedded in later buildings but you'll notice its similarity to Porta Palatina in Turin. Arco Augusto, dating from BC9, commemorates a truce with the local Celts. An aqueduct, Terme Graziane, was built toward the end of Roman rule. The Cathedral San Giusto, built in the 11th century, retains its Romanesque bell tower, as well as later Gothic features and fine carved wooden choir stalls.

Sauze d'Oulx

Three mountain peaks soar above this small resort town, where pioneer downhill skiers paved the way for the freestyle and men's and women's mogul competitions of the 2006 Olympics. World Cup and Olympic gold medal slalom skier Piero Gros grew up here. 🌐 www.comune.sauzedoulx.to.it 🅰 Exit the A32 onto S24 at Oulx, well signposted.

Cesana Torinese

The group of small villages huddle in mountain passes includes Cesana, the largest, San Sicaro and Monte Fraitève, 5 km (3 miles) higher up Monte Fraitève. The trip from Oulx to Claviere (S24) follows the valley of the river Dora Riparia into a land of hidden

▶ *Soaring peaks overlook the Olympic resort of Sauze d'Oulx*

valleys.The alpine skiing, freestyle downhill and combined, super-G, biathalon, relays, bobsleigh, luge and skeleton of the 2006 Olympics led to improvements in the skiing facilities.

ⓐ Cesana, San Sicaro. ⓦ www.comune.cesana.to.it

Bardonecchia

A warren of medieval houses fills the old town of this ski resort snuggled up against the French border and at the foot of massive mountains. A 12 km (7.5 mile) tunnel, Traforo di Frejus, bores through the mountain to Mondane, in France. South of town on Colomion (2100 m/6500 ft), La Selletta (2230 m/6900 ft) and on the flanks of Mt Jefferau (2807m/8700 ft) east of it, ski slopes provide the trails used for the snowboard, giant slalom, half-pipe and snowboard cross competitions of the 2006 Olympics. When not used for Olympics the area is known for beginner-friendly trails: 18 trails for intermediate skiers and ten for beginners. Facilities include Nordic trails, ice skating, ice climbing, snow-shoeing and snowmobiling.

ⓦ www.comune.bardonecchia.to.it/turismo.htm.

Val del Chisone

Running between Pinerolo, southwest of Turin, and Sestriere, the valley of the Chisone River goes through Parco Naturale della Troncea and past the ski resort of Pregelato. The fastest way there might be the Corso Regina Margarite to the A32 west to Oulx, then following the S24 and S23. The other alternative from Turin is to follow Via Sacchi, which becomes Corso Federico Turati, to S23 and on to Pinerolo, at the eastern end of the valley. Pinerolo is site of the curling competitions of the 2006 Winter Olympics. ⓐ Turismo Viale Giolitti, Pinerolo.

ⓣ 0121.794.003. ⓦ www.montagnedoc.it

Pragelato

Another tiny town, this one is famed for its Nordic skiing. Regularly groomed ski trails and walking paths head from town into the Parco Naturale della Troncea. Rent mountain bikes at **Il Fouia**, a hotel/bar in La Rua (❶ 0122.788.84) or **Pizzeria Il Mulino** in the village of Plan (❶ 0122.780.02). The ski jump, built for the men's ski jumping competitions of the 2006 Olympics and used for the 2005 World Cup, provides for additional winter sport opportunities. The town also has an indoor swimming pool.

Parco Naturale della Troncea

Following the Chisone River, the park spreads onto the surrounding hillsides. Several attractive walking, hiking and mountain bike trails are in the park, mapped in 22 itineraries, from easy to difficult. One leads to where copper was mined in the 19th century, until the site and the town were abandoned in the 1920s. The park is home to deer, ibex, boar, wolves, fox, ermine and bird life, and the visitor centre has a small museum with displays on these and on its mining history. ❸ Via della Pineta Fraz Rua, Pragelato. ❶ 0122.788.49. ❿ www.parconaturalevaltroncea.it

Sestriere

This town is one of the grand old places of Italian skiing, a legacy of FIAT's Giovanni Agnelli who, in the 1930s, decided to build four cable cars, ski facilities and a pair of hotels at the foot of the mountains. As one of the earliest ski resorts, it has the most facilities and the richest clientele of the Susa-Chisone ski areas, but it's nothing to look at (unless you count people-watching). The 2006 downhill, freestyle and combined downhill, special combined, and men's and women's slalom and giant slalom were not the first time world ski

figures have skied here. In addition to skiing, the winter offers bobsledding, heli-skiing and dog sledding – take lessons at **Scuola Italiani Conductori Cani di Slitta** (🕿 012.283.2473). Summer activities include hiking, climbing, mountain biking and golf at Europe's highest course, **Sestrieres Golf Club** (🕿 012.275.5170). 🛈 Turismo Via Lousett. Ⓦ www.comune.sestriere.to.it

CULTURE

The great outdoors and mountain sports are the draw in these towns, but a few interesting museums are worth a stop if you have time. Hours at these tend to be erratic, so its best to call unless you're driving right past.

Forte de Exilles
From very early times there has been an important fortress here, protecting the region from invasions from the north. The massive fort was such a pain in the side of Napoleon that he ordered it destroyed. Shortly after he gave up his Italian kingdom it was rebuilt and has since been restored, now housing a museum of the history and culture of the Alpine region.
🛈 Exilles. Ⓦ www.fortificazioni.com/exilles.html.
🕘 Tues–Sun 10.00–19.00 (May–Sept) Fri–Sun 10.00–17.00 (Oct, Mar–Apr). 🚗 Access from the S335 or A32 west of Susa.

Museo Etnologico
The little home-grown museum interprets life in the Alpine valleys through old farm implements and household items. 🛈 Via des Geneys 6, Bardonecchia. 🕿 012.290.2612, 🕘 Mon–Fri 09.00–12.30, 15.00–19.00 (July–Aug); Sat–Sun, holidays: 09.00–1230, 15.00–19.00

Museo d'Arte Preistorica

Unique in the scope of its collections – it covers prehistoric rock art throughout Europe – this museum gives a window into prehistoric art from the Neolithic to the Iron Age. ❸ Viale Giolitti 1, Pinerolo. ❶ 012.179.4382. Ⓦ www.cesmap.it

Museo del Costume delle Tradizioni delle Genti Alpine

Glimpse into the lives of the rugged mountain people that have populated these towns for generations, through the clothing and tools used in their daily lives. ❸ Via San Giovanni, Borgata Rivetta, Pragelato. ❶ 012.278.800. ◷ Daily Aug; Sat–Sun Sept–July. Admission charge.

RETAIL THERAPY

The latest skiwear, woodcarvings and local edibles and drinkables are the prime shopping subjects here, along with climbing and hiking gear in the summer. Bardonecchia's main street is lined with shops offering hand-made wooden carvings, and in the Cesana Torinese towns look for the herb liqueur, salamis and toma cheeses that these towns are noted for.

Don't pass through Avigliana without tasting – and stocking up on – *baci al cioccolato* and *Aviglianesi al rhum*, both delectable sweets. Serious resort shoppers need to go straight to Sestriere, where shops around the Piazza Fraiteve clothe the very well-heeled and trendy.

TAKING A BREAK

Surprisingly, food at the trailside cafés and snack bars is quite cheap and good, and pizzerias abound for the budget-minded. By late

▲ *Take home some traditional Piedmontese woodcraft*

afternoon, skiers have begun to fill the cafés and bars, many of which serve snacks with drinks.

Italian Mega-pizzas, cheap prices, friendly atmosphere.
ⓐ Via Medial, Bardonecchia.

Cafe Medail A pleasant staff, good quick pick-me-ups and drinks.
ⓐ Via Stazione 2, Bardonecchia. ⓣ 0122.999.844.

Filanda The show is as good as the finished pizza. ⓐ Via Medail 100, Bardonecchia. ⓣ 0122.999.780.

AFTER DARK

Don't expect a tourist-style club scene in quiet Bardonecchia, but if you're willing to join in with the local life, ask where the rock bands Schiffida and Derrymain are playing. *Après-ski* lasts most of the night in Sauze d'Oulx, where Via Assietta is lined with bars and pubs.

Things really heat up in très-chichi Sestiere – if the town were more attractive, you might mistake it for Courmayeur (or St Moritz) from the clientele and the bars and cafés around Piazza Fraiteve. Drinks are expensive, but the snacks are generous.

Gina – Il Bandito Nightly live music and shows, loud and active. ⓐ Piazzale Miramonti 10, Sauze d'Oulx. ⓣ 012.285.0671.

Wine Bar Gran Trun Good wine list, nice environment, and light food. ⓐ Via Assietta 37, Sauze d'Oulx. ⓣ 012.285.0016.

Schuss Disco Dance till dawn at this hold-over from the original disco era, still going loud and strong after 40 years. ⓐ Via Clotes 1, Sauze d'Oulx. ⓣ 012.285.0194.

Restaurants

Bardosteria €–€€ The chef is fussy about using locally produced organic ingredients. The gigantic *Gran Plateau di Formaggi* is like a ploughman's lunch on steroids. ⓐ Via Medail 33, Bardonecchia. ⓣ 012.299.862.

Du Grand Pere €€ In a 17th-century house, this attractive restaurant serves well-prepared traditional fare. ⓐ Via Forte Seguin 14, Sestriere. ⓣ 012.275.5970.

Ristorante Bar Biovey €€ With well-prepared and ample servings, this chef-owned dining room is several cuts above the usual ski resort dining. ⓐ Via Generale Cantore (near the lower Jafferau lift station), Bardonecchia. ⓣ 0122.999.215. Closed Tues.

Restaurante Stazione €€ Sample Piemontese specialties, such as *arrosto al fieno Savoiardo* (meat roasted and infused with aromas of alpine flowers). ⓐ Corso Stati Uniti 4-6, Susa. ⓣ 012 2262 2226.

Il Cantun del Barbabuc €€–€€€ Regional dishes using locally produced ingredients. Soups are especially good here. ⓐ Via Luigi Faure 3, Sauze d'Oulx. ⓣ 012.285.8593.

Il Capricorno €€€ This may well be the best restaurant in town, and in winter they'll bring you there by snowmobile. ⓐ Via Case Sparse 21, Sauze d'Oulx. ⓣ 0122.850.273. ⓦ www.chaletilcapricorno.it

ACCOMMODATION

Lodging options vary from luxury hotels – especially in Sestriere – to village B&Bs and cosy chalets on mountainsides close to ski lifts. In Sestriere, many hotels close in summer. Avoid August, unless you reserve early, when half of Turin empties into these mountain resorts.

THE VIA LATTEA

Literally, the Milky Way, this system of ski trails covers the upper parts of the Susa and Chisone valleys and criss-crosses the border between Italy and France. The system encompasses more than 400 km (250 miles) of Alpine and Nordic trails with numerous cable cars, chair lifts and T-bars. Snow shoeing, ice-skating, heli-skiing and snowmobiling are available within the system, and lodgings can be arranged so skiers need not return to a base every night. ⓦ www.vialattea.it

Hotel Napoleon € The Napoleon is located in the centre of town and has been run by the Vanara family since 1970. A bit austere on the outside, it is attractive, bright and comfortable inside and good value. ⓐ Via Mazzini 44, Susa. ⓣ 012.262.2855. ⓕ 012. 231.900. ⓦ www.hotelnapoleon.it

La Posta € The three rooms in this B&B are freshly renovated, with private baths, TV, private entrances. ⓐ Via Nazionale, 15 Fraz. La Ruà , Pragelato. ⓣ/ⓕ 012.278.940, mobile: 349.454.1573.

Hotel Betulla €–€€ All 40 modern rooms in this chalet-style building, close to skiing, have TV, many have balconies. ⓐ Viale della Vittoria 400, Bardonecchia. ⓣ 0122.999.846. ⓦ www.mediturhotels.it

Hotel Bucaneve €–€€ Although it is a larger hotel, it has welcoming public spaces and offers a covered swimming pool. ⓐ Viale della Vecchia, 2, Bardonecchia, ⓣ 012.299.9892, ⓕ 012.299.9980. ⓦ www.hotelbucanevebardonecchia.it

Hotel Sciatori €€ The 25-room alpine chalet offers bed and breakfast, half- or full-board. ⓐ Via S. Filippo 5, Borgata Sestriere. ⓣ 012.270.323, ⓕ 012.270.196. ⓦ www.hotelsciatorisestriere.it

Il Capricorno €€ Modern and very comfortable, this seven-room inn is close to the Pian della Rocca chairlift. ⓐ Via Casc Sparse 21, Sauze d'Oulx. ⓣ 012.285.0273. ⓕ 012.285.0055. ⓦ www.chaletilcapricorno.it

Grand Hotel Principi di Piemonte €€–€€€ The modern hotel with fitness facilities and Turkish bath is close to the Via Lattea. ⓐ Via Sauze 3, Sestriere. ⓣ 012.275.5333. ⓕ 012. 275.5411.

Gran Paradiso & the Val d'Aosta

Just north of Turin, at the boundary between the Piedmont and Val d'Aosta regions, is Italy's oldest national park, the 70,010 hectare (173,000-acre) Gran Paradiso. Like so many other of the region's treasures, it was a legacy of the Savoys, who donated their 2023-hectare (5000-acre) hunting reserve in 1919 as its nucleus. Beyond its ever-white peaks is the richly historic Val d'Aosta, a major trade and military route since the Celts, and Rome's northernmost outpost two millennia ago. It's a land of castles (about 100 of them), Roman remains, Gothic art, green meadows of wildflowers, crystal lakes and world-class ski resorts.

SIGHTS & ATTRACTIONS

The very fact that it is at the foot of three of Europe's most famous peaks – Mont Blanc, Monta Rosa and the Matterhorn – should make the Val d'Aosta one of Italy's most visited regions, but quite the opposite is true. Although the route down the narrow valley of the Dora Baltea River was heavily travelled in antiquity – the Roman way-station at Aosta grew to such splendour that Aosta was called the 'Rome of the Alps' – today it is the playground of skiers and hikers, but not many others. The old Roman road has been replaced by the S26 and paralleled by the A5 autostrada, which affords stunning views as it whisks cars from Turin to the Mont Blanc tunnel. Nothing is far from these two roads, which will form the spine of your travel route.

Gran Paradiso National Park – south

No roads cross the wall formed by 4061-metre (12,590 ft) Mt Gran Paradiso, rising at the border of Piedmont and Val d'Aosta regions.

Roads and tracks from the south lead to hiking trails and mountain *rifugios*; this southern part of the park will interest outdoors enthusiasts and climbers, who can get information at the visitors centre in Noasca. ⓐ Segreteria turistica del Parco. Noasca, Valle Orco. ☏ 0124.901.070. ⏱ year round.

Gran Paradiso National Park – north

Those interested in more than hiking should go to the park's northern sector, reached from the A5 near Aosta. The few roads that penetrate the park's wilderness follow valleys, ending at remote villages and hamlets, most of which have seasonal visitors centres that include small museums. From these villages, trails climb to views of rocky peaks inhabited by illusive ibex and chamois. Ⓝ Trains almost hourly from Turin's Porta Susa station to Aosta. Buses to valleys in the park: SVAP ☏ 800.256.552 or 0165.411.25. Ⓦ www.svap.it SAVDA ☏ 0165.262.027. Ⓦ www.savda.it

Cogne

Cogne sits at the end of a valley, with views of broad green meadows and a wall of white-topped mountains. On all sides are the rocky cliffs that characterise these Alpine peaks. Like many Val d'Aosta towns, bilingual Cogne seems as French as it is Italian. Even deeper into the mountains, at the end of the valley is tiny Lillaz, where Cascata di Lillaz drops in a series of long waterfalls, a short walk from the village. Hiking trails into the park begin here and from nearby Valnontry, where there is park information at Giardino Alpino Paradisia, an alpine garden with local plants labelled and described. A half-day hike leads from the garden to the mountain

▶ *Val d'Aosta is watched over by magnificent Mont Blanc*

rifugio at Vittorio Sella, passing the farmhouses of Herbetet and magnificent views of glaciers. This is a trip for good weather only, as the path is quite open. ⓐ Giardino Alpino Paradisia ⓣ 0165.741.47. ⓦ www.parks.it ⓛ June–Sept.

Monte Cervino (Matterhorn)

It is ironic that arguably the ugliest of all Alpine resorts sits in one of the Alps' most beautiful locations. The Matterhorn, known to Italians as Cervino, is even more dramatic from the Italian side than it is in its iconic Swiss setting, but Zermatt has done far better by it. You still need to go all the way to Breuil-Cervenia to board cable cars to its upper slopes, but stop first at Lago Bleu, a few kilometres before town. Its waters mirror the mountain, whose distinctive shape rises straight ahead, framed in trees. Benches are thoughtfully provided for picnickers.

ⓐ Turismo Via J. A. Carrel 29, Cervinia. ⓣ 0166.949.136.

Courmayeur and Monte Bianco

Although it is right under Europe's mightiest piece of rock, Monti Bianco (Mont Blanc) the actual mountain is hidden from view in Courmayeur by a smaller, closer peak. But the scenery from its high (literally) street is still good. The glamour is the town's main attraction, apart from its location, although the Alpine museum (see page 136) is worth a stop.

ⓐ Turismo Piazzale Monte Bianco 13, Courmayeur. ⓣ 0165.842.060.

Funivia del Monte Bianco

On a clear day, few experiences in Europe beat the cable car trip up 3225 m (10,000ft) high. Punta Helbronner on the French border, or riding on, suspended over the glacier, to the ski resort of Chamonix,

France. The ride begins at La Palud, 4 km (2 miles) from Courmayeur.
ⓐ Entreves. ⓣ 0165.846.658. ⓦ www.courmayeur-montblanc.com
ⓛ early July–late Aug.

Roman sites

Roman walls still encircle the Romans' Augusta Praetoria, now
Aosta, with guard towers still standing. But even more impressive
are the well-preserved Arch of Augustus and the Roman theatre, of
which an entire wall still stands after just short of 2000 years.
Burrowing beneath the city are catacombs; a map of Roman Aosta is
free at the tourist information office (where there is a 21st-century
free internet point). An archaeological museum (see page 134) helps
paint the picture of the city in Roman times.
ⓐ Turismo Pza Chanoux 8. ⓣ 0165.236.627.

Sant' Orso

Aosta's monastic complex that just kept growing over the centuries
is a catalogue of successive artistic styles, distributed among its
church, bell tower, cloister and crypts. The highlight is the cloister,
with its fine stone carving on its columns.ⓐ V. Sant'Orso, Aosta.
ⓣ 0165 262026. ⓛ Tues–Sat 09.00–19.00, Sun 12.00–19.00; winter:
Mon–Sat 09.30–12.00 and 14.00–17.30, Sun 14.00–17.30.

Castles

The Dora Baltea's upper valley has an astonishing number of castles
for an area of its size. In various stages of repair, from over-restored
to crumbling, more than 80 of them once defended the valley from
invaders or collected tolls from passing merchants and pilgrims.
Today these provide a moody backdrop to little towns and good
photo-opportunities. Below Aosta are the fortifications that spill

from hilltop Bard and the 15th-century Issogne castle, a short walk from the Verrès train station. Aymavilles has a tiny turreted 14th-century castle and Verrès is considered one of Europe's best examples of late Gothic military building. Some, including Fenis and Sarre are restored or contain museums.

CULTURE

No museum in the Val d'Aosta comes close to outshining Turin's wealth of them, but several are of note to those with special interests, and the restored Fenis Castle is worth a stop. Tourist office: ⓐ **AIAT** Castello di Sarre. ⓣ 0165.257.854. ⓦ www.granparadiso.net. ⓛ July–Aug Mon–Sat 08.30–12.30, 14.00–18.00, Sun 08.30–12.30, Dec–June closed Wed pm, Sun.

Museo Archeologico

Despite its many Roman buildings, Aosta is not rich in Roman treasure – it has been on too many invasion routes. But it has enough for a very good museum, which interprets the bronzes, busts, chalices, crosses, tombstones and bone art from Neolithic through medieval times. ⓐ Pza Roncas 1, Aosta. ⓣ 0165.238.680. ⓛ Daily 09.00–19.00.

Museo dall'Ospizia

At the top of the Gran San Barnardo Pass, 35km (22 miles) from Aosta (longer by the older and more scenic road) is a showy panorama of snow-capped mountains. Just over the Swiss border is a museum about the monk who built the first travellers' hospice, and

▶ *Just the place to shop for souvenirs of your stay – Cogne*

for whom both the pass and the breed of rescue dogs were named.
One or two of the dogs are usually on hand (but without kegs).
❶ (41) 787.1236. **◷** Daily 08.00–19.30 mid-June–mid-Oct.

Museo Alpina Duca degli Abruzzi

The Alpine Guides Society of Courmayeur has restored their historic
Guides House to contain a museum of Alpine climbing and life.
Along with historical artifacts and memorabilia is an excellent
display of mountain photography. **❷** Piazza Henry 2, Courmayeur.
❶ 0165.842.064. **◷** Tues–Sun 09.30–18.30.

Castello Reale

Built in 1710 on the foundations of a 13th-century fortified manor,
the castle became the hunting lodge of Italy's last king, Umberto
and it was here that his wife, Princess Maria Jose, was sent with the
children after her unsuccessful attempt to secure a separate peace
between Italy and the USA during World War II.
❷ Sarre. **❶** 0165.257.539. **◷** Tues–Sun 10.00–12.30, 13.30–17.30, Sun
10.00–12.30, 13.30–18.00. Admission charged.

Castello di Fenis

The restored castle has a lovely 15th-century courtyard with a curved
stairway rising to wooden balconies. The courtyard and chapel are
painted in *freschi*, most in excellent condition. **❷** Fenis. **❶** 0165.764.263.
◷ Daily 09.00–19.00 mid-Mar–June and Sept; 09.00–20.00 July–Aug.

RETAIL THERAPY

With its abundance of forests, the Val d'Aosta is known for its fine
woodcarving. Ths takes the form of both traditional pieces and

thoroughly contemporary designs in kitchen-ware and household decor. Cogne is a particular centre, with several shops selling toys, Christmas ornaments, kitchen utensils and decorative sculptures. Courmayeur is the place to find the latest ski and sportswear as well as trendy fashions. A wide variety of local products, from wines and pasta to the famous local wildflower honey are displayed in small shops and boutiques along Aosta's Via San Ansalmo.

Cogne

Da Mastro Geppetto Woodenware Christmas decorations and toys by a master craftsman. ⓐ Via Bougeois 1, Cogne. ⓣ 0165.749.156

IVAT Wrought iron, baskets and woodcarving, in elegant contemporary and traditional styles. ⓐ Rue Dr Grappein 32, Cogne. ⓣ 0165.743. 22.

Les Amis du Bois A co-operative shop owned by local master woodcarvers. ⓐ Fraz. Villes Dessus 9, Introd (16 km/10 miles from Aosta). ⓣ 0165.955.57.

TAKING A BREAK

The mountain refuges (*rifugios*) offer hearty hot soups to skiers in winter and full meals for hikers in the summer. The tourist office in Aosta has a list of these, as do the park information offices. All the ski resort towns, as well as Aosta, have plenty of cafés.

Rifugio Vittorio Sella This *rifugio* is in the Lauson Valley, about 2.5 hours' walk from the alpine garden, a good destination for a morning hike. ⓐ Fraz. Valnontey, Cogne. ⓣ 0165.743.10.

Ⓦ www.rifugiosella.com Ⓛ Daily 12.30–15.00 and 19.15–21.00 late Mar–late Sept.

Pizzeria du Tunnel Rustic Usually crowded and really good pizza. Ⓐ Via Circonvallazione, Courmayeur. Ⓣ 0165.841.705.

Pizzaria Trattoria Lou Hand-made pizza and traditional hearty mountain dishes. Ⓐ Fraz. Epinel 27b, Cogne. Ⓣ 0165.751.973. Ⓛ Daily 12.30–14.00, 19.30–22.00; closed Thurs in off seasons.

AFTER DARK

Courmayeur's population of high-altitude high rollers brings nightlife, and prices to match, but if you brought your trendiest sportswear (this season's, please) you can promenade or lounge in the cafés to watch Fifi and Mimi parade past with their owners, on jewelled leashes. The upside of this pretty cluster of jetset habitats is that the restaurants are very good. While nightlife exists –if you ask around you can find the current place to dance till dawn – Courmayeur is not exactly the best resort for party animals. At most of the ski resort towns, the action is in the *après-ski* hours, which tend to begin early and last well into the evening. Expect bars with the classiest clientele – such as Courmayeur's Cadran Solaire and Bar Roma – to have ritzier prices, but to lay on free snacks. Cheese fondue is a favourite après-ski dish.

Restaurants
Osteria Trattoria Cretaz €–€€ Local ingredients, such as venison with blueberries, distinguish this homey osteria. Ⓐ Fraz. Cretaz, Cogne. Ⓣ 0165.746.51. Ⓛ 12.00–14.00, 19.00–21.30, closed Wed in low season.

La Cave de Tillier Ristorante Brasserie €–€€ Tender potato gnocchi in creamy fontina cheese sauce is the house specialty first course at this cheery steakhouse. ➌ Via de Tillier 40, Aosta. ➊ 0165.230.133.

Ristorante Praetoria €–€€ Polenta is a local specialty, served here with rabbit. ➋ Via San Anselmo 9. ➊ 0165.443.56.

La Clusaz Locanda Ristorante €€€ Extraordinary cuisine, based on seasonal ingredients, served *prix fixe*. Starter options include their own cured meats. ➌ Gignod (SS27 on the way to the Gran San Bernardo pass). ➊ 0165.560.75. ➍ www.laclusaz.it ➎ Daily, except lunch Tues–Wed.

Clubs, bars & discos
Planet Disco Bar Late-night option with a DJ – not a good choice if you plan on first tracks in the morning. ➌ Centro Sportivo, Plan des Lizzes, Courmayeur. ➊ 0165.844.409.

Fashion Café DJ music until all hours, with a lively and friendly crowd. ➌ Località Amérique 17, Aosta. ➊ 349.329.8221 ➎ 23.00–05.00 Fri–Sat.

ACCOMMODATION

Lodgings in the Val d'Aosta range from rustic mountain *rifugios*, or hikers' dorms, to beautiful and luxurious grand hotels. In between these are modest *alberghi* and charming *locande*, often owned by a talented chef whose dining room makes the *locanda* a destination. As you might expect, the upper-end hotels cluster in classier resorts like Courmayeur.

Rifugio Vittorio Sella € The rifugio, which sleeps 160 hikers, was once a hunting lodge of King Vittorio Emanuele II. It is about 2.5 hours' walk from the alpine garden. ⓐ Fraz. Valnontey, Cogne. ⓣ 0165.743.10. ⓦ www.rifugiosella.com ⓛ Late Mar–late Sept.

Hotel Miage €€ Small hotel with views, in-room TVs, parking and a restaurant. ⓐ Via Ponte Suaz 137, Aosta. ⓣ 0165.238.585. ⓕ 0165.236.355.

Bellevue €€–€€€ The view is superb, overlooking the green (or white) valley with mountains all around. Good restaurant and an indoor swimming pool. ⓐ Rue Grand Paradis 22, Cogne. ⓣ 0165.748.25. ⓦ www.hotelbellevue.it

Hotel Europe €€–€€€ Modern hotel in the historic centre, a few steps from the main piazza and Roman sites and a short walk from the train station. Covered parking, free internet access and a welcoming staff. ⓐ Piazza Narbonne 8, Aosta 11100. ⓣ 0165.236.363. ⓦ www.ethotels.com

Romantik Hotel Villa Novecento €€€ Luxuriously appointed and individually decorated rooms in a restored mansion, with sauna, whirlpool tubs and fitness centre.ⓐ Viale Monte Bianco 64, Courmayeur. ⓣ 0165.843.000. ⓦ www.villanovecento.it

---

▶ *The rack railway to Basilica di Superga*

Directory

GETTING THERE

Turin's location in northern Italy, close to Milan, makes it easily accessible from anywhere in Europe – or the world. Depending on where you begin, the options include air, rail, bus and car, or a combination of these.

By air

From the UK and Europe Ryanair (ⓦ www. ryanair.com) flies daily from Stansted to Turin's Sandro Pertini (Caselle) airport, often at ridiculously low fares. EasyJet (ⓦ www.easyjet.com) serves Turin directly from Luton and British Airways (ⓦ www.britishairways.com) has two daily flights direct to Turin from Gatwick. Alitalia (ⓦ www.alitalia.com) flies the same route with competitive fares. Ryanair also flies direct to Turin from Orly in Paris, and most major airports offer flights to Turin via national carriers. Connections are also possible via Milan and Genoa. Milan Malpensa has a direct bus to Turin (see page 47) and Genoa is only an hour by train.

From North America There are no direct flights to Turin from the USA or Canada, but several airlines fly from major US gateways to Milan's Malpensa airport, connected to Turin by direct shuttle or by an easy train connection via Milan's Stazione Centrale (ⓦ www.trenitalia.it).

From Australia and New Zealand No direct flights are offered to any Italian city, so the best plan is to book the best price to a major European hub, with an onward connection to Turin or Milan.

Although there are fewer ready-made packages to Turin than to resort holiday havens, you can sometimes combine air fare, lodging and car hire into a money-saving package. Ask about the possibilities when booking flights. Especially when booking an entire package, it is wise to secure your trip with travel insurance. Most tour operators offer insurance options, or you can insure the trip independently to protect your investment.

By train

With the arrival of Eurostar Italia services, Turin's Porta Susa station becomes a rail direct link between Geneva and Milan, so a rail trip from London's Waterloo Station to Turin now takes just over 11 hours. Less pricey are conventional trains connecting from Milan, Genoa or Lyon. Turin is on the main line from Paris to Milan. Travel time is 4 hours from Paris by Eurocity service, 6 hours by slower train, and 1 hour 40 minutes from Milan. Italian trains run on time (www.trenitalia.it). Be sure to have your ticket date-stamped in a machine on the platform of the station before boarding.

Travellers from outside Europe who plan to use trains should investigate the various multi-day train passes on Trenitalia and multi-country travel offered by Rail Europe. For travellers anywhere, Rail Europe offers a one-stop source of information, reservations and tickets.

The monthly *Thomas Cook European Rail Timetable* has up-to-date schedules for European international and national train services.

Trenitalia Ⓦ www.trenitalia.it

Rail Europe Ⓦ www.raileurope.com

Thomas Cook European Rail Timetable ☏ (UK) 01733 416477; (USA) 1 800 322 3834). Ⓦ www.thomascookpublishing.com

By bus

Barring a lucky hit at a cut-rate air fare, the cheapest way to Turin from the UK is by bus, about 24 hours from London's Victoria Coach

Station via Eurolines UK (☎ 08705 143219. ⓦ www.gobycoach.com or www.eurolines.com).

By road

The Mont Blanc Tunnel speeds the trip across the Alps into the Piedmont along the A5 autostrada. The other major route across the Alps is from Lyon, through Chambery, France, via the Trafero del Frejus tunnel. Driving time from Lyon or Zurich is about 4 hours. Italy, like the rest of the continent, drives on the right-hand side of the road.

⬇ *It's the common currency for most of Europe*

ENTRY FORMALITIES

Visa requirements

UK citizens with a valid passport may stay without a visa for an unlimited period. Citizens of the Republic of Ireland, USA, Canada, New Zealand, Australia, Singapore and Israel need only a valid passport to enter Italy and do not require visas for stays of up to 90 days. Citizens of South Africa must have visas to enter Italy.

Customs

EU citizens can bring goods for personal use when arriving from another EU country, but must observe the limits on tobacco (800 cigarettes) and spirits (10 litres over 22 per cent alcohol, 90 litres of wine). Limits for non-EU nationals are 200 cigarettes and one litre of spirits, two of wine.

MONEY

The euro (€)is the official currency in Italy. €1 = 100 cents. It comes in notes of €5, €10, €20, €50, €100, €200 and €500. Coins are in denominations of €1 and €2, and 1, 2, 5, 10, 20 and 50 cents.

Currency exchange facilities and ATMs are near the arrival gates at both Caselle and Malpensa airports.

Avoid carrying large amounts of cash, and if you must, hide it well in several concealed pockets and security pouches. Safer are traveller's cheques, accepted at banks, large hotels and by larger stores, but difficult to cash elsewhere. If possible, bring at least one major credit card; Visa is the most commonly accepted. Most small hotels, *agriturismo* properties and small restaurants do not accept cards.

Best for obtaining euros are credit or debit cards. Automated teller machines (*bancomat*) offer the best exchange rates, are found

even in small towns and never close. Ask your card issuer before leaving home what network you can use in Italy and make sure that your PIN number can be used abroad. Banks are usually open Mon–Fri 08.30–13.00 or 13.30. Try to have enough euros to last over weekends, when banks close and ATMs may be out of money or out of order. Try to arrive with euros, especially on a weekend.

HEALTH, SAFETY & CRIME

While you need to be aware of your surroundings in any city, and avoid walking alone at night and in seedy neighbourhoods, Turin is not particularly dangerous for travellers. Guard against pickpockets by carrying (well hidden) only the cash you need. Waist packs and bum bags label you as a tourist and make you a particular target anywhere. Be especially wary of crowded areas, such as train stations, buses and street markets, and avoid groups of small children who try to engage you in conversation. They are fast and work expertly in teams. Keep cameras firmly in your hand and the strap around your neck. As anywhere, don't leave cameras or handbags slung over the back of your chair. This said, petty theft is not especially common in Turin.

Report any thefts immediately, and be sure to get a copy of the report (*denuncia*) for insurance. Police are of two varieties, the *carabinieri*, or national police, and the *vigili*, or local officers. Both are armed and can make arrests, but the *vigili* are usually more concerned with traffic and parking. They normally wear white uniforms in the summer, black in the winter. You can report a crime to either, but the paperwork must be completed at a *questura* (police station).

Drinking water is safe in Turin, as is food; it is wise to carry your favourite medication for upset stomach, since travellers anywhere are more likely to eat and drink things their systems are unaccustomed to. Should you become ill or have an accident, medical care is quite good and free to EU residents who carry a European Health Insurance Card. Non-EU residents should carry travellers health insurance if their own coverage does not cover re-imbursement, and should also consider emergency medical evacuation insurance. Emergency treatment at hospitals is free to everyone. For police and medical emergency numbers, see Emergencies, page 156).

As a pedestrian, always look both ways when crossing even on one-way streets, since bus lanes sometimes travel in the opposite direction. Those from left-hand drive countries need to be especially careful because traffic will be approaching from an unfamiliar direction. There are fewer motorised two-wheeled vehicles here than in most Italian cities, but you should always be aware of these approaching between vehicles or emerging suddenly from alleyways.

OPENING HOURS

Major attractions open 08.30 or 09.00 to 19.00 or 19.30 with Monday closing. Smaller ones may have shorter hours, frequently closing for lunch. Hours are subject to change, so ask at the tourist office for the most up-to-date times (websites are notoriously out of date).

Banks open Mon–Fri 08.30–13.00 or 13.30. Shops generally open 09.00 or 10.00 until 19.00 or 19.30 Mon–Sat, sometimes with an hour or two closing at lunch and Monday morning closing (Tuesday for food shops). Sunday openings are becoming more common.

Street markets open about 07.00 and close around midday. Pharmacies are usually open Mon–Sat 08.00–13.00 and

16.00–20.00, and a sign on the door will direct you to the nearest one open Sundays and nights.

TOILETS

Public buildings, such as museums, usually have clean toilets in the publicly accessible areas near the entrance (or will let you in to use one if you look desperate), and you will find occasional public facilities in the centre of the city (Piazza Solferino's is in the Atrium). But the fastest and easiest solution is to step into a bar or café and go directly to the back, following the sign 'toilet' or the universal symbols. These may not be entirely savoury affairs (always carry your own paper), but they are available. At public toilets, be prepared to pay a small fee, usually €0.50.

CHILDREN

Italians love children – and spoil them – but in Turin rarely take them out to dinner in the evening, especially to classier restaurants. These will not have appropriate chairs or children's portions and the staff may relegate you to a corner near the kitchen. Better to choose a small neighbourhood trattoria, where your whole family will be welcomed. Hotels can usually provide cots with advance notice, and you will rarely be charged for a child staying in a room with adults. Special infant needs, such as baby food and nappies, are available in supermarkets, but for a shorter stay it is easier to bring familiar brands from home.

Turin has a number of child-friendly sights and activities on offer. Rides appealing to children include noisy, lumbering trams (children under 1m/3 ft tall ride free), the Mole's glass elevator and the rack railway climbing to Superga, across the river. Borgo Medioevale is a low-key, free mock-medieval village, complete with an armour shop, and frequent hands-on activities for children (ask if any are scheduled that day).

🔻 *Turin is a great place for children to explore*

Older children will appreciate the mummies and other Egyptian relics in the Egyptian Museum and the creepy tunnels of the Museo Pietro Micca. In addition to the elevator in the Mole, that building houses the excellent cinema museum, with sets and props from famous films, plus animation exhibits.

Across the river, the abandoned zoo becomes Experimenta in summer, a science experience centre with plenty of activities for all ages. ❸ Corso Casale 15. ☎ 800.329.329. 🌐 www.experimenta.to.it 🕐 June–mid-Sept 16.00–24.00 Mon-Sat, all day Sun; mid-Sept–Oct 15.00–20.00 Tues–Sat, all day Sun. Admission charged. Ⓝ Bus/tram 3, 61,75.

COMMUNICATIONS
Phones

All Turin numbers begin with 011, which must be dialed from inside or outside the city. Numbers vary between 8 and 9 digits, with a few shorter ones remaining. Numbers beginning with 800 are toll-free. To use public telephones, buy a card (*carta telefonica*) from a *tabacchi*, designated by a white T on a dark background. Hotel telephones usually carry a high surcharge, but not always, so ask at the desk.

To make an international call, dial 00, then the country code (UK 44, Republic of Ireland 353, US and Canada 1, Australia 61, New Zealand 64, South Africa 27) and number, omitting the initial zero in UK numbers. To call Turin from outside Italy, dial the international access code (00 in the UK and Ireland, 011 in the US), then Italy's country code of 39, then the number (which will be prefixed with 011 for Turin).

Mobile phone numbers begin with 3; if you see an old number with the prefix 03, omit the zero. UK, New Zealand and Australian mobile phones will work in Italy; US and Canadian cell phones will not.

Post

The Italian postal service, despite what you may have heard, is quite reliable. For letters and post cards you can buy stamps at *tabacchi*, and for special services you can go to a post office at Via Alfieri 10 in central Turin or at Via Nizza 10, behind Porta Nuova station. If you pay extra for *prioritaria*, your card or letter should arrive the next day in Italy, within three days in the UK and about five days elsewhere. Rates change often, so check at the *tabacchi* selling the stamps.

Internet

Internet access is increasingly available, both in hotels and internet points and cafés around the city. Most upper-end hotels have in-room points, others will likely allow you to plug into their phone systems. Tourist information office and kiosks can provide lists of internet cafés and public access points such as libraries.

ELECTRICITY

Electrical appliances used in the UK will work in Italy, but those from the US and Canada will need an adapter to convert from 110v to 220v. Plugs are two- or three-pin, round pin types.

TRAVELLERS WITH DISABILITIES

The building boom for the Olympics has helped to improve facilities for the disabled in Turin, since new buildings must meet the new standards for wheelchair access. While the law does require Turin restaurants to have both tables and toilets accessible to wheelchairs, in practice most do not. A good bet are the restaurants

in modern buildings, such as the Lingotto and those in hotels. A call in advance can determine what is available. Major sites with ramped access, lifts and suitable toilets include the Egyptian and cinema museums, GAM (the modern art museum), the Agnelli gallery in the Lingotto complex and Rivoli Palace. Turismo Torino, in the Atrium – itself wheelchair accessible – can provide current lists.

The entire bus system is being upgraded to include access for the disabled, and some tram lines (4 and 10 among them) are already fitted. Some cars on trains from the airport have wheelchair access. Most trains have access, but you must reserve at least 24 hours in advance and go about an hour early to fill in forms. Each station (in theory) has an *Officio Disabili* and many have specially outfitted waiting rooms for wheelchair passengers.

Call a taxi ahead to be sure of having one with space for a folded wheelchair, or call the special taxi service for those with disabilities (☎ 011.581.16). Most public toilets have special wheelchair facilities. For current information before leaving home, contact RADAR (⌂ 12 City Forum, 250 City Rd, London EC1V 8AF. ☎ 071.250.3222. ⓦ www.radar.org.uk).

TOURIST INFORMATION
Tourist offices
Turismo Torino ☎ 011.535.181. 🖷 011.530.070.
ⓔ info@turismotorino.org ⓦ www.turismotorino.org

Information points
Atrium Torino ⌂ Piazza Solferino ⏲ Daily 09.30–19.00.
Information Turismo ⌂ Porta Nuova railway station.
⏲ Mon–Sat 09.30–19.00, Sun 09.30–15.00.
Information Turismo ⌂ Caselle airport. ⏲ Daily 08.30–22.30.

Useful websites

Ⓦ **www.turismotorino.org** The official and very useful site of Turismo Torino, with extensive listings of attractions, dining, entertainment and other information, many with map locations, all in English.

Ⓦ **www.extratorino.it** Another excellent and easy-to-navigate site with useful details on attractions, dining, shopping and more, in English.

Ⓦ **www.torino2006.org** Everything about the Olympics, including information and updates on venues and events.

Ⓦ **www.piemondo.it** Information on the entire Piedmont region, with useful links and information on lodging and travel.

Ⓦ **www.italiantourism.com** The Italian national tourism (Ente Nazionale Italiano per il Turismo, or ENIT) site, with general information on travel in Italy, as well as regional coverage.

Italian Overseas Tourist Offices

Italian State Tourist Office ⓐ 1 Princes Street, London W1R 8AY, UK. ℹ (020) 7408 1254. Ⓦ www.piuitalia2000.it

Italian Government Tourist Board ⓐ 630 Fifth Ave, Suite 1565, New York, NY 10111, USA. ℹ (212) 245 5618.

Italian Government Tourist Board ⓐ 175 Bloor Street East, Suite 907, South Tower, Toronto, ON M4W 3R8, Canada. ℹ (416) 925 4882. Brochures: ℹ (416) 925 3870.

Italian Government Tourist Office ⓐ 44 Market St, Level 6, Sydney NSW 2000, Australia. ℹ (02) 9262 1666. Ⓦ www.italiantourism.com.au

Italian Tourist Office ⓐ Italian Embassy, 796 George Avenue, Arcadia 0083, Pretoria, South Africa. ℹ (012) 430 5541.

Italian Tourist Office ⓐ Italian Embassy, 34–38 Grant Road, Thorndon, Wellington, NZ. ℹ (04) 4947 173.

Useful phrases

Although English is spoken in many tourist locations in Turin, these words and phrases may come in handy. See also the phrases for specific situations in other parts of this book.

English	Italian	Approx. pronunciation
BASICS		
Yes	Sì	See
No	Noh	Noh
Please	Per favore	Perr fahvawreh
Thank you	Grazie	Grahtsyeh
Hello	Salve	Sahlveh
Goodbye	Arrivederci	Arreevehderrchee
Excuse me	Chiedo scusa	Kyehdaw skooza
Sorry	Scusi	Skoozee
That's okay	Va bene	Vah behneh
To	A	Ah
From	Da	Dah
I don't speak Italian	Non parlo italiano	Nawn parrlaw itahlyahnaw
Do you speak English	Parla inglese?	Parrla eenglehzeh?
Good morning	Buon giorno	Booawn geeyawrnaw
Good afternoon	Buon pomeriggio	Booawn pawmehreehdjaw
Good evening	Buona sera	Booawnah sehrah
Goodnight	Buona notte	Booawnah nawtteh
My name is ...	Mi chiamo ...	Mee kyahmaw ...
DAYS & TIMES		
Monday	Lunedì	Loonehdee
Tuesday	Martedì	Marrtehdee
Wednesday	Mercoledì	Merrcawlehdee
Thursday	Giovedì	Jawvehdee
Friday	Venerdì	Venerrdee
Saturday	Sabato	Sahbahtaw
Sunday	Domenica	Dawmehneeca
Morning	Mattino	Mahtteenaw
Afternoon	Pomeriggio	Pawmehreedjaw
Evening	Sera	Sehra
Night	Notte	Notteh
Yesterday	Ieri	Yeree

English	Italian	Approx. pronunciation
Today	Oggi	Odjee
Tomorrow	Domani	Dawmahnee
What time is it?	Che ore sono?	Keh awreh sawnaw?
It is ...	Sono le ...	Sawnaw leh ...
09.00	Nove	Noveh
Midday	Mezzogiorno	Metsawjorrnaw
Midnight	Mezzanotte	Metsanotteh

NUMBERS

One	Uno	Oonaw
Two	Due	Dweh
Three	Tre	Treh
Four	Quattro	Kwahttraw
Five	Cinque	Cheenkweh
Six	Sei	Say
Seven	Sette	Setteh
Eight	Otto	Ottaw
Nine	Nove	Noveh
Ten	Dieci	Dyehchee
Eleven	Undici	Oondeechee
Twelve	Dodici	Dawdeechee
Twenty	Venti	Ventee
Fifty	Cinquanta	Cheenkwahnta
One hundred	Cento	Chentaw

MONEY

I would like to change these traveller's cheques/this currency	Vorrei cambiare questi assegni turistici/ questa valuta	Vawrray cahmbyahreh kwestee assenee tooree-steechee/kwesta vahloota
Where is the nearest ATM?	Dov'è il bancomat più vicino?	Dawveh eel bankomaht pyoo veecheenaw?
Do you accept credit cards?	Accettate carte di credito?	Achetahteh kahrrteh dee krehdeehtaw?

SIGNS & NOTICES

Airport	Aeroporto	Ahaerrhawpawrrtaw
Rail station	Stazione ferroviaria	Stahtsyawneh ferrawvyarya
Platform	Binario	Binahriaw
Smoking/non-smoking	Per fumatori/ non fumatori	Perr foomahtawree/ non foomahtawree
Toilets	Bagni	Banyee
Ladies/Gentlemen	Signore/Signori	Seenyawreh/Seenyawree
Subway	Metropolitana	Metrawpawleetahna

Emergencies

POLICE

Should you need to report a theft, missing person or any other matter for the police, go to the *questura*, or police station, not far from Porta Susa station. If insurance is involved, ask for a *denuncia*, a stamped form that you must have for filing claims. Questura. ❸ Corso Vinzaglio 10. ❶ 011.558.81. To reach the police in an emergency: ❶ 112.

MEDICAL

Should you become ill while traveling, you have several sources of information on English-speaking doctors. If you can reach your consulate, they can provide a list, or you can go prepared with the appropriate pages from the directory published by IAMAT. The International Association of Medical Assistance for travellers is a non-profit organisation that provides medical information on health-related travel issues all over the world, as well as a list of English speaking doctors (Ⓦ www.iamat.org).

Hospital accident and emergency departments, (ask for the *pronto soccorso*) are open 24-hours daily, and must treat you free of charge in an emergency. Several hospitals are grouped in Turin's Lingotto neighbourhood, some with specialties. For an emergency medical team or ambulance: ❶ 113.

Ospedale Infantile Regina Margherita (Women's and children's hospital) ❶ Piazza Polonia 94; Pronto Soccorso, Via Zuretti 23. ❶ 011.313.4444. Ⓦ www.oirmsantanna.piemonte.it ❶ Ⓝ Bus/tram 1, 18, 74, 34, 35, 42.
Azienda Sanitaria Ospedaliera San Giovanni Battista ❸ Corso Bramante 88/90. ❶ 011.633.1633, Pronto Soccorso 011.633.5248

l'Ospedale Maria Vittoria ❸ Via Cibrario 72, Pronto Soccorso Corso
Tassoni, 46. ℹ 011.439.3111. Ⓝ Bus/tram 9, 13, 16, 71.

CONSULATES & EMBASSIES

British Consulate General ❸ Via S. Paolo 7, 20121 Milano.
ℹ 02.723.001, afteroffice hours: 335. 810.6857. ℹ 02.864.65081.
Ⓦ www.britishembassy.gov.uk/italy

American Consulate General ❸ Via Principe Amedeo 2, 20121 Milano.
ℹ 02.626.88520. ℹ 02.659.6561. Ⓦ www.usembassy.it

Australian Consulate General ❸ 3rd Floor, Via Borgogna 2, 20122 Milano.
ℹ 02.777.041. ℹ 02 777.04242. Ⓦ www.australian-embassy.it

New Zealand Embassy ❸ Via Zara 28, 00198 Roma. ℹ06.4417171,
ℹ 06.440.2984.

South African Consul General ❸ Vicolo S.Giovanni sul Muro 4, 20121
Milano. ℹ 02.885.8581,www.sudafrica.it

Embassy of Canada, Consular Section ❸ Via Zara 30, 00198 Roma.
ℹ 06.445.981; automated information line: 06.445.983.937.
ℹ 06.445.983.750.

EMERGENCY PHRASES

Help! Aiuto! *Ahyootaw!*   **Fire!** Al fuoco! *Ahl fooawcaw!*
Stop! Ferma! *Fairmah!*

Call an ambulance/a doctor/the police/the fire service!
Chiamate un'ambulanza/un medico/la polizia/i pompieri!
Kyahmahteh oon ahmboolahntsa/ oon mehdeecaw/la
pawleetsya/ee pompee-ehree!

A

accommodation 32–37;
 see also hotels
Agnelli family 18, 104
air connections 46–47,
 142–143
airports 46–47
Aosta 133, 134
Armeria Reale 63
art nouveau 80–81, 82
Artillery Museum 83
arts 18–20
Aymavilles 134

B

banks 146
Bard 134
Bardonecchia 119
Basilica di Superga 102
Biblioteca Reale 58
bicerin 88
boat trips 100
Borgo Medioevale 98
bus connections 47,
 143–144

C

cafés 66–69, 86–89,
 106–107, 109–110,
 123–124
Cappella della Pia
 Congregazione dei
 Banchieri e dei
 Mercanti 78
car hire 54
Casa Fossati Rayneri 76
Castello de Fenis 136
Castello della Mandria 114
Castello di Rivolli 113
Castello Reale, Sarre 136
Castello Valentino 97
Cathedral 72–74
Cesana Torinese 118
children 148–150
Cineman Museum 103
Cittadella 72–93

climate 8
clubs, bars & discos
 28–29, 71, 92–93, 112,
 124–125, 139
Cogne 130–132, 137
Consolata, La 77
consulates & embassies
 157
Corpus Domini church 76
Courmayeur 132, 136
credit cards 145
Cremagliera, La 102
culture 18–20
currency 145
customs regulations 145
cycling 31

D

disabilities, travellers
 with 151–152
driving 47, 144
Duomo di San Giovanni
 Battista 72–74

E

Egyptian Museum 64
electricity 151
emergencies 156–157
entertainment 28–29
events 8–11

F

Fenis 136
festivals 8–11, 43
food & drink 24–27
football 30
Forte de Exilles 122

G

Galleria Civica d'Arte
 Moderna e
 Contemporanea (GAM)
 84
Galleria Sabauda 65
GAM 84
gay movement 17
Giardini Reali 58–59

Gran Madre di Dio church
 100–101
Gran Paradiso 128–140
Gran Paradiso National
 Park 128–130

H

health 146–147, 156
history 14–15
Holy Shroud of Turin 72,
 81–83
hotels
 Alpine areas 126–127
 Turin 32–37
 Val d'Aosta 139–140

I

internet cafés 151

L

language 154–155
lifestyle 16–17
Lingotto Complex, 30, 100

M

Matterhorn 132
Mole Antonelliana 94–96
money 145–146
Monte Bianco 132–133
Monte Cervino 132
Mountain Museum
 104–105
Murazzi 96
Museo Alpina Duca degli
 Abruzzi, Courmayeur
 136
Museo Archeologico,
 Aosta 134
Museo Civico Pietro
 Micca 83
Museo d'Arte Preistorica,
 Pinerolo 123
Museo dall'Ospizia
 134–136
Museo del Costume delle
 Tradizioni delle Genti
 Alpine, Pragelato 123

Museo dell'Automobile 103–104
Museo della Marionetta Piemontese 84, 92
Museo della Sindone 81–83
Museo di Antichità 81
Museo di Arti Decorative 109
Museo Egizio 64
Museo Etnologico, Bardonecchia 122
Museo Nazionale del Cinema 103
Museo Nazionale del Risorgimento Italiano 64
Museo Nazionale della Montagna 104–105
Museo Storico Nazionale dell'Artigliera 83
music 28–29, 110

N
nightlife 28–29

O
Olympics 116
opening hours 147
orientation 48
Orto Botanico 97–98

P
Palazzina di Caccia di Stupinigi 113
Palazzo Carignano 60
Palazzo Falletti di Barolo 78
Palazzo Madama 59–60
Palazzo Reale 58, 62–63
Parco Naturale della Troncea 120
Parco Regionale La Mandria 114
Parco Valentino 97
parking 48
passports & visas 145

phones 150
Piazza Castello 56–58
Piazza Consolata 77
Piazza San Carlo 60–62
Piazza Solferino 80
Piazza Vittorio Veneto 96
Pinacoteca Agnelli 104
Po, River 94
police 156
Porta Palatina 74–76
post 151
Pragelato 119–120
public holidays 11
public transport 49–54

Q
Quadrilatero 72–93

R
rail connections 47, 143
rail station 47
Reggia di Venaria Reale 114
restaurants 26–27, 125–126, 138–139
Risorgimento 15, 64
riverside area, Turin 94–114
road connections 144
Rocca Medioevale 98
Roman remains 74–76, 133
Royal Armoury 63
Royal Library 58
Royal Palace 58, 62–63
royal palaces 113–114

S
Sacra di San Michele 116
safety 48, 146–147
San Domenico church 77
San Francesco church 79–80
San Lorenzo church 59
San Massimo church 96–97
Sant'Orso 133

Santa Maria del Monte church 101
Santuario di Santa Maria Consolatrice 77
Sarre 136
Sauze d'Oulx 118
Savoy Centre 56–71
Savoy, House of 14, 18
seasons 8
Sestriere 120–122
shopping 22–23, 65–66, 84–86, 105–106, 123, 136–137
skiing see winter sports
slow food 11, 24, 105
sport 30–31
Susa 118

T
taxis 54
Teatro Regio 63–64
Teatro Romano 74
theatres 69–71, 92, 110
time differences 46
tipping 27
toilets 148
Torino Card 52
tourist information 152–153
Turin Shroud 72, 81–83

V
Val d'Aosta 128–140
Val del Chisone 119
Verrès 134
Via Garibaldi 78
Via Lattea ski trails 126
Via Po 62

W
weather 8
wine 25
wine bars 42
Winter Olympics 2006 12–13
winter sports 12–13, 30, 116, 126

The publishers would like to thank the following individuals and organisations for supplying their copyright photographs for this book. Stillman Rogers Photography: all photographs except : A1 Pix: page 119; Jolly Hotels: page 36; Turismo Turino: pages 5, 45 (Veronica Rossi); 7 (Michele d'Ottavio); 19 (Museo Nazionale del Cinema); 21, 85 (Giuseppe Bressi); 31 (Pinacoteca Giovanni & Marella Agnelli); 87 (Roberto Borgo & Pierandrea Monni); 91 (EPAT); 112 (Regione Piemonte); 115 (Montagne DOC); 70, 141; Torino 2006 XX Olympic Winter Games: page 13.

Copy editor: Deborah Parker
Proofreader: Stuart McLaren

Send your thoughts to
books@thomascook.com

- **Found a great bar, club, shop or must-see sight that we don't feature?**

- **Like to tip us off about any information that needs a little updating?**

- **Want to tell us what you love about this handy little guidebook and more importantly how we can make it even handier?**

Then here's your chance to tell all! Send us ideas, discoveries and recommendations today and then look out for your valuable input in the next edition of this title. As an extra 'thank you' from Thomas Cook Publishing, you'll be automatically entered into our exciting monthly prize draw.

Email to the above address (stating the book's title) or write to: CitySpots Project Editor, Thomas Cook Publishing, PO Box 227, Unit 15/16, Coningsby Road, Peterborough PE3 8SB, UK.